Inner Dimensions of the Salāh

"If you wish to check how much you love Allah, then see how much your heart loves the Quran, and you will know the answer."

Al-Imam Ibn Al-Qayyim

Copyright

King Fahd Complex for Printing

Editor/Writer: Noah Ibn Kathir, Imam Ahamd, Imam Ibn Al-Qayyim

All rights reserved. No part of this book may be reproduced or transmitted in any form or by any means, electronic or mechanical, including photocopying, recording, or by any information storage and retrieval system, without written permission from the Publisher.

Contents

"The keys to the life of the heart lie in reflecting upon the Quran, being humble before Allah in secret, and leaving sins."

Introduction ... 9
   Ibn Al-Qayyim ... 10
      His Manners and Worship ... 12
      His Death ... 14

Chapter One ... 15
   The Salah is Allah's gift to the believers ... 16
   The Likeness of the Heart to the Earth ... 22
   Heart turns dry when devoid of tawhid ... 25
   Actions of the limbs ... 29
   Parable in Three Types of People ... 32
   The Secret and Essence of Salah ... 37
   The detachment from Allah ... 40
   Discussion on Wudu ... 42

Attending the Mosque ... 43

Servitude in al-Takbir ... 45

Servitude in al-Istiftah ... 47

Ibn Taymiyyah's advice to Ibn Qayyim ... 51

The State of the 'abd in al-Fatihah ... 53

The meanings of Al-hamd ... 54

Servitude in "Lord of all the worlds" ... 61

Servitude in "The Merciful (al-Rahmān) ...62

"Master of the Day of Judgment" ... 64

The meanings of Thanā and Tamjid ... 65

Servitude in "You Alone we worship" ... 67

The wisdom behind al-Isti'ānah ... 69

The Straight Path ... 72

Servitude in raising the hands ... 77

Servitude in al-Ruku' ... 79

Servitude in Al-Qiyām ... 81

Servitude in Al-Sugud ... 82

The Salah is built upon five pillars ... 85

The State of between the 2 Prostrations ...90

The Second Prostration ... 93

Al-Tashahhud and Al-Tahiyyat ... 97

The Noblest words after the Quran ... 103

Servitude in al-Taslim ... 104

The two Shahadahs in al-Tahiyyat ... 106

Sending al-Salat upon the Prophet ... 108

The Sunnah of the Adhan ... 109

Chapter Two ... 113

Devotion in Salah ... 114

Discussion on Taslim ... 121

Exposition on the fruits al-Khushu ... 123

True devotion to Allah ... 125

Why Salah gives us comfort? ... 127

Benefits of Salah is nearness to Allah ... 130

Chapter Three …135

Distinction between the people of al-Samā and the people of Salah

Chapter Four …139

Al-Sama' of the people of Truth … 143

Chapter Five …149

The Types of Hearts

Appendix One …161

Al-Imam Ibn al-Qayyim on Khushu

Appendix Two …169

Al-Imam Ibn al-Qayyim on Hypocritical Khushu

"Whoever prefers Allah to all others, Allah will prefer him to others."

Books by Ibn Kathir & Ibn Al-Qayyim

"The sinner does not feel any remorse over his sins, that is because his heart is already dead"

* Stories of the Prophets
  ISBN 9798774942602
* Seerah of Prophet Mūhammad
  ISBN 9781094860213
* Stories of the Koran
  ISBN 9781095900796
* The Path to Guidance
  ISBN 9781643540818
* Purification of the Soul – Vol 1
  ISBN 9781643541389
* Tafseer Ibn Kathir
  ISBN 9781512266573
* Al-Fawaid: Wise Sayings
  ISBN 9781727812718

* Heaven's Door
ISBN 9781643541396
* The Ideal Muslimah by *Ibn Kathir*
ISBN 9798834334422
* Koran: English Easy to Read
ISBN 9781643540924
* Characteristics of Hypocrites
ISBN 9781643541358
* Diseases of the Hearts
and their Cures
ISBN 9781643541129
* Tawbah: Turning To Allah
ISBN 979-8517657411
* The Holy Quran – Clear and
Easy to Read: in English
ISBN 979851591373
* Timeless Seeds of Advice
ISBN 9798784652522

Introduction

Successful indeed are the believers: those who are humble in their prayer. And they who turn away from ill speech. [And they who are observant of Zakat. And who guard their modesty. [23:1-5]

قَدْ أَفْلَحَ ٱلْمُؤْمِنُونَ ۝

ٱلَّذِينَ هُمْ فِى صَلَاتِهِمْ خَٰشِعُونَ ۝

وَٱلَّذِينَ هُمْ عَنِ ٱللَّغْوِ مُعْرِضُونَ ۝

وَٱلَّذِينَ هُمْ لِلزَّكَوٰةِ فَٰعِلُونَ ۝

وَٱلَّذِينَ هُمْ لِفُرُوجِهِمْ حَٰفِظُونَ ۝

O you who believe! Bow down, and prostrate yourselves, and worship your Lord and do good that you may be successful. [22:77]

يَٰٓأَيُّهَا ٱلَّذِينَ ءَامَنُوا۟ ٱرْكَعُوا۟ وَٱسْجُدُوا۟ وَٱعْبُدُوا۟ رَبَّكُمْ وَٱفْعَلُوا۟ ٱلْخَيْرَ لَعَلَّكُمْ تُفْلِحُونَ ۝

And whosoever obeys Allah and His Messenger (SAW), fears Allah, and keeps his duty (to Him), such are the successful ones. [24:52]

وَمَن يُطِعِ ٱللَّهَ وَرَسُولَهُۥ وَيَخْشَ ٱللَّهَ وَيَتَّقْهِ فَأُوْلَٰٓئِكَ هُمُ ٱلْفَآئِزُونَ ۝

But as for one who had repented, believed, and done righteousness, it is promised by Allah that he will be among the successful. [28:67]

فَأَمَّا مَن تَابَ وَءَامَنَ وَعَمِلَ صَٰلِحًا فَعَسَىٰٓ أَن يَكُونَ مِنَ ٱلْمُفْلِحِينَ ۝

Ibn Al-Qayyim

Shams ad-Din Mūhammad ibn Abi Bakr ibn Qayyim al-Jawziyyah was born in 691H / 1292 CE in az-Zur'i, a small village 55 miles from Damascus. Very little is known of his childhood except that he received a comprehensive Islamic education thanks to the fact that his father was principle of the School al-Jawziyyah.

This Madrasah was one of the few centers devoted to the study of Hanbali fiqh in Damascus. After completing his studies at the Jawziyyah, Ibn Al-Qayyim continued his learning in the circles of the shaykhs who filled the city's mosques. It appears that for some period of time, he came under the influence of Mu'tazili teachings and probably of certain mystics. In the epic-length Ode he wrote in later years, he refers to this period as being one of confusion and misguidance: *"All these [ways] did I try, and I fell into a net, fluttering like a bird that knows not where to fly."*

From an early age he set about acquiring knowledge of the Islamic sciences from the scholars of his time. He had an intense love for books and knowledge. He acquired from such books what others could not acquire, and he developed a deep understanding of the books.

The most notable of his teachers was Imam Ibn Taymiyyah. He accompanied and studied under for sixteen years. He attained great proficiency in many branches of knowledge; particularly knowledge of Tafsir and Hiadith. He became a unique scholar in many branches of knowledge.

His Manners and Worship

Many of his students and contemporaries have born witness to his excellent character and his manners of worship. Ibn Rajab said: "He was constant in worship and performing the night prayer, reaching the limits in lengthening his prayer and devotion. He was constantly in a state of dhikr and had an intense love for Allah. He also had a deep love for turning to Allah in repentance, humbling himself to Him with a deep sense of humility and helplessness.

He would throw himself at the doors of Divine obedience and servitude. Indeed, I have not seen the likes of him with regards to such matters."

Ibn Kathir said: "He was constant in humbly entreating and calling upon his Lord. He recited well and had fine manners. He had a great deal of love and did not harbour any envy or malice towards anyone, nor did he seek to harm or find fault with them. I was one of those who most often kept company with him and was one of the most beloved of people to him. I do not know of anyone in the world in this time, who is a greater worshipper than him. His prayer used to be very lengthy, with prolonged bowing and prostrations. His colleagues would criticize him for this, yet he never retorted back, nor did he abandon this practice. May Allah bestow His mercy upon him.

His Death

Imam ibn Al-Qayyim passed away at the age of sixty, on the 13th night of Rajab, 751H, may Allah shower His Mercy upon him.

Ibn Qayyim Al-Jawziyya Sayings

"There is no joy for the one who does not bear sadness, there is no sweetness for the one who does not have patience, there is no delight for the one who does not suffer, and there is no relaxation for the one who does not endure fatigue."

"Every love that leads away from His love is in fact a punishment; only a love that leads to His love is a heartfelt and pure love."

Chapter One

In the name of Allah, the Entirely Merciful, the Especially Merciful

Al-Imam Ibn Qayyim al-Jawziyyah, may Allah bestow His Mercy upon him, said: "This is a discourse on the inclination towards listening to music and songs versus the affinity to Salah and the Quran - offering a detailed account of how the experience derived from the Quran and Salah is antithetic to that of music and singing. It will also elucidate the inverse relation between the two inclinations and the manner in which the strength and influence of one necessities the weakness and ineffectiveness of the other, the stronger the yearning for music and singing is, the weaker shall the attachment to Salah and Quran. *And the worldly life is not but amusement and diversion; but the* home of the Hereafter is best for those who fear Allah, so will you not reason? [6:32]*

وَمَا ٱلْحَيَوٰةُ ٱلدُّنْيَآ إِلَّا لَعِبٌ وَلَهْوٌ ۖ وَلَلدَّارُ ٱلْءَاخِرَةُ خَيْرٌ لِّلَّذِينَ يَتَّقُونَ ۗ أَفَلَا تَعْقِلُونَ ۝

Prayer (the Salah) is Allah's gift to the believers. It is tranquility for worshippers

It is imperative for you to know that Salah is, without any doubt, the domain of tranquility for devotees, the enjoyment of the souls of monotheists, the garden of the worshippers, the essence of enjoyment of the humble ones, the test of the sincere ones, and the scale measuring the mettle of those embarking the right path.

And keep up prayer and pay the poor-rate and bow down with those who bow down. [2:43]

وَأَقِيمُوا۟ ٱلصَّلَوٰةَ وَءَاتُوا۟ ٱلزَّكَوٰةَ وَٱرْكَعُوا۟ مَعَ ٱلرَّٰكِعِينَ ۝

It is truly a divine Mercy that Allah has gifted to His believing servants that He has guided them to, and acquainted them with. He delegated His truthful and honest Messenger, Prophet Mūhammad, peace and blessing be upon him, to deliver this gift to His believing servants in order that they may attain a noble status with Him.

Through its means He dignifies, honours and showers them with His Mercy, and allows them to win His nearness. He bestows upon His believing servants all this although He is in no need of them, He just wants to lavish them with this gracious gift to show His favour upon them and bring their hearts and bodies altogether into His servitude. He, the Most Exalted, endows the heart of the knower of Allah1 by enabling him to reap the best of its harvest; turning to Him, Exalted be He, rejoicing in His closeness, basking in His love, enjoying standing before Him [in Salah], dismissing everything except Him [from his heart] as soon as he commences worship, and fulfilling the rights of his servitude to Him, inwardly and outwardly, in order for his worship to be in a manner that pleases Allah. *And keep up prayer and pay the poor-rate and whatever good you send before for yourselves, you shall find it with Allah; surely Allah sees what you do. [2:110]*

﴿وَأَقِيمُواْ ٱلصَّلَوٰةَ وَءَاتُواْ ٱلزَّكَوٰةَ وَمَا تُقَدِّمُواْ لِأَنفُسِكُم مِّنْ خَيْرٍ تَجِدُوهُ عِندَ ٱللَّهِ إِنَّ ٱللَّهَ بِمَا تَعْمَلُونَ بَصِيرٌ ۝﴾

Even as Allah tested His servants by creating them with innate lusts and desires and exposing them to external temptations, His Mercy and Kindness mandated that Allah, the Most High, give His servants a feast comprising of several kinds of delicacies, nourishments, gifts and grants [to help them repel these desires and temptations]. And He did invite them to attend this banquet on a daily basis not once, but five times a day, and he distinguished each served course of this banquet with a unique flavour and a special benefit to perfect the pleasures and complement the benefits they attain, and (help them to) perfect their servitude to Allah. Thus, not only did He make every act of worship performed in Salah a means of remedy to atone for the (minor) sins they committed, but rewarded them with a special light for praying. *Men whom neither trade nor sale diverts them from the Remembrance of Allah (with heart and tongue), nor from performing As-Salat (Iqamat-as-Salat), nor from giving the Zakat. They fear a Day when hearts and eyes will be overturned (from the horror of the torment of the Day of Resurrection). [24:37]*

رِجَالٌ لَّا تُلْهِيهِمْ تِجَٰرَةٌ وَلَا بَيْعٌ عَن ذِكْرِ ٱللَّهِ وَإِقَامِ ٱلصَّلَوٰةِ وَإِيتَآءِ ٱلزَّكَوٰةِ يَخَافُونَ يَوْمًا تَتَقَلَّبُ فِيهِ ٱلْقُلُوبُ وَٱلْأَبْصَٰرُ ﴿٣٧﴾

In fact, Salah brings forth light and strength into the heart, increases the share of one's provision in this life, inspires others to love the one who prays, and lets Angels and also the earth with its mountains, trees and rivers rejoice. Furthermore, on the Day of Judgment, when the believing servants [of Allah] meet their Lord, their Salah shall turn into light and transform into reward. Before attending the feast their hearts endured starvation, thirst and nakedness but as soon as they commence the worship [i.e. Salah], all that shall change to become the opposite, hence they shall leave the feast with stomachs full, throats moistened and bodies attired. *Indeed, your Lord knows, that you stand [in prayer] almost two thirds of the night or half of it or a third of it, and [so do] a group of those with you. And Allah determines [the extent of] the night and the day. He has known that you [Muslims] will not be able to do it and has turned to you in forgiveness, so recite what is easy [for you] of the Qur'an. He has known that there will be among you those who are ill and others traveling throughout the land seeking [something] of the bounty of Allah and others fighting for the cause of Allah. So recite what is easy from it and establish prayer and give zakah and loan Allah a goodly loan. And whatever good you put forward for yourselves - you will find it with Allah. It is better and greater in reward. And seek forgiveness of Allah. Indeed, Allah is Forgiving and Merciful. [73:20]*

﴿ إِنَّ رَبَّكَ يَعْلَمُ أَنَّكَ تَقُومُ أَدْنَىٰ مِن ثُلُثَيِ ٱلَّيْلِ وَنِصْفَهُۥ وَثُلُثَهُۥ وَطَآئِفَةٌ مِّنَ ٱلَّذِينَ مَعَكَ ۚ وَٱللَّهُ يُقَدِّرُ ٱلَّيْلَ وَٱلنَّهَارَ ۚ عَلِمَ أَن لَّن تُحْصُوهُ فَتَابَ عَلَيْكُمْ ۖ فَٱقْرَءُوا۟ مَا تَيَسَّرَ مِنَ ٱلْقُرْءَانِ ۚ عَلِمَ أَن سَيَكُونُ مِنكُم مَّرْضَىٰ ۙ وَءَاخَرُونَ يَضْرِبُونَ فِى ٱلْأَرْضِ يَبْتَغُونَ مِن فَضْلِ ٱللَّهِ ۙ وَءَاخَرُونَ يُقَٰتِلُونَ فِى سَبِيلِ ٱللَّهِ ۖ فَٱقْرَءُوا۟ مَا تَيَسَّرَ مِنْهُ ۚ وَأَقِيمُوا۟ ٱلصَّلَوٰةَ وَءَاتُوا۟ ٱلزَّكَوٰةَ وَأَقْرِضُوا۟ ٱللَّهَ قَرْضًا حَسَنًا ۚ وَمَا تُقَدِّمُوا۟ لِأَنفُسِكُم مِّنْ خَيْرٍ تَجِدُوهُ عِندَ ٱللَّهِ هُوَ خَيْرًا وَأَعْظَمَ أَجْرًا ۚ وَٱسْتَغْفِرُوا۟ ٱللَّهَ ۖ إِنَّ ٱللَّهَ غَفُورٌ رَّحِيمٌۢ ﴿٢٠﴾

The Likeness of the Heart to the Earth

Due to the sterility and poverty [of indolence, disaffection, idleness, etc.] that the hearts and souls endure time and time after, the invitation is renewed five times a day. However, the Mercy of Allah necessitated that a gap of time pass between each invitation so the invitee is constantly calling for the rain from the One in whose Hand is the water to quench the hearts, and beseeching the clouds of His Mercy to have their water descend upon his heart in order that the trees of Eman and the harvest of Ihsan, growing from this divine Mercy, do not dry out. *Whoever desires the harvest of the Hereafter - We increase for him in his harvest. And whoever desires the harvest of this world - We give him thereof, but there is not for him in the Hereafter any share. [42:20]*

مَن كَانَ يُرِيدُ حَرْثَ ٱلْأَخِرَةِ نَزِدْ لَهُۥ فِى حَرْثِهِۦ وَمَن كَانَ يُرِيدُ حَرْثَ ٱلدُّنْيَا نُؤْتِهِۦ مِنْهَا وَمَا لَهُۥ فِى ٱلْأَخِرَةِ مِن نَّصِيبٍ ۝

The essence of these plants maintains their survival in his heart and his soul; therefore the heart of the 'abd (of Allah) continues to implore in humility for the rain (to fall upon his heart) from his Lord and invoke Him to relieve his heart from drought and thirst. This truly for the 'abd of Allah is the way of life.

Indeed, those who believed and those who were Jews or Christians or Sabeans [before Prophet Mūhammad] - those [among them] who believed in Allah and the Last Day and did righteousness - will have their reward with their Lord, and no fear will there be concerning them, nor will they grieve. [2:62]

إِنَّ ٱلَّذِينَ ءَامَنُواْ وَٱلَّذِينَ هَادُواْ وَٱلنَّصَرَىٰ وَٱلصَّبِـِٔينَ مَنْ ءَامَنَ بِٱللَّهِ وَٱلْيَوْمِ ٱلْأَخِرِ وَعَمِلَ صَلِحًا فَلَهُمْ أَجْرُهُمْ عِندَ رَبِّهِمْ وَلَا خَوْفٌ عَلَيْهِمْ وَلَا هُمْ يَحْزَنُونَ ۝

Indeed, the drought of hearts is heedlessness, but as long as the 'abd (of Allah) is indulged in the remembrance of Allah and constantly turning to Him, the rains of His Mercy will shower his heart abundantly.

As soon as he becomes heedless however, drought shall strike his heart and the damage caused will be according to the degree of his heedlessness. This is because when thoughtlessness dominates and overwhelms the heart, its land becomes lifeless; it shall produce no harvest for reaping, and the fire of desires will scorch it from every side, leaving the land bare after it had once been rich with every different kind of vegetation.

And We send down blessed rain from the sky and made grow thereby gardens. [50:9]

وَنَزَّلْنَا مِنَ ٱلسَّمَآءِ مَآءً مُّبَٰرَكًا فَأَنۢبَتۡنَا بِهِۦ جَنَّٰتٖ وَحَبَّ ٱلۡحَصِيدِ ﴿٩﴾

But as soon as the rains of Mercy fall upon the heart of the 'abd (of Allah), the land of his Eman and deeds quivers, turns fertile causing every lovely kind to grow thereon, sustained and nourished by the life-giving water. When the land is deprived of water, the branches and leaves of its flora wither away, becoming fruitless; even the branches are bereft of benefit as they become rigid and fragile.

At this juncture, the wisdom of the One overseeing this garden dictates having these dried trees cut and making its wood a fuel for fire.

The heart turns dry when devoid of tawhid

Similarly is the case with the heart of the 'abd (of Allah), it becomes very dry whenever it is devoid of:

1) Love for Allah

2) Knowledge about Him
3) His remembrance (dhikr)
4) Supplication and invocation
5) Most importantly, tawhid

Allah is your Lord! La ilaha illa Huwa (none has the right to be worshipped but He), the Creator of all things. So worship Him (Alone), and He is the Wakil (Trustee, Disposer of affairs, Guardian, etc.) over all things. [6:102]

ذَٰلِكُمُ ٱللَّهُ رَبُّكُمْ لَآ إِلَٰهَ إِلَّا هُوَ خَٰلِقُ كُلِّ شَىْءٍ فَٱعْبُدُوهُ وَهُوَ عَلَىٰ كُلِّ شَىْءٍ وَكِيلٌ ﴿١٠٢﴾

This is because the heat of desire and the fires of lust (shahwa) infiltrating the heart cause the branches (i.e. limbs) to become unresponsive, inflexible and inert (whenever the 'abd of Allah intends to employ them in good deeds). Under these circumstances, the tree including its branches is rendered useless.

Its only fitting use is as fuel for (Hell) fire. Allah said: *So is one whose breast Allah has expanded to [accept] Islam and he is upon a light from his Lord [like one whose heart rejects it]? Then woe to those whose hearts are hardened against the remembrance of Allah. Those are in manifest error. [39:22]*

أَفَمَن شَرَحَ ٱللَّهُ صَدْرَهُۥ لِلْإِسْلَٰمِ فَهُوَ عَلَىٰ نُورٍ مِّن رَّبِّهِۦ ۚ فَوَيْلٌ لِّلْقَٰسِيَةِ قُلُوبُهُم مِّن ذِكْرِ ٱللَّهِ ۚ أُو۟لَٰٓئِكَ فِى ضَلَٰلٍ مُّبِينٍ ﴿٢٢﴾

When the heart is watered with the rains of Mercy, the branches will be soft, moist, pliable and responsive; if you call them for the worship of Allah, they submit and hasten to obey, letting you reap from each branch the fruits of (true) enslavement to Allah, whose essence is the irrigation of the heart, which influences (the functioning of) the heart and the limbs.

On the other hand, when the heart is parched and dried (i.e. rigid and hardened), the branches do not perform any good deeds because the essence of life is missing from the heart, thus the limbs are cut off from life accordingly. And even though each limb has been created and pre- pared to render a unique act of worship demonstrating an aspect of mankind's servitude to Allah, the limbs cannot produce their anticipated harvest due to the incapacity and hindrance in their functioning.

Know that the life of this world is but amusement and diversion and adornment and boasting to one another and competition in increase of wealth and children - like the example of a rain whose [resulting] plant growth pleases the tillers; then it dries and you see it turned yellow; then it becomes [scattered] debris.

And in the Hereafter is severe punishment and forgiveness from Allah and approval. And what is the worldly life except the enjoyment of delusion. [57:20]

Divisions of People in regards to the actions of the limbs

In light of this, people are of three kinds in regards to the actions of their limbs:

1) Those whose limbs are engaged in the service of their Lord, to fulfill the purpose for which they are created. They are among the successful 'merchants' who have made Allah's obedience to be their trade and livelihood, from which they yield the greatest profits. Salah has been prescribed in such a manner, that the entire body follows the lead of the heart- so that each limb practices its individual act of worship demonstrating its servitude to Allah.

These are the category of people who have realized the grace of Allah upon them and have understood the true purpose behind the creation of their limbs, and therefore they dedicate their limbs to worshipping their Lord, all the while safeguarding them from being involved in matters that may displease Him - so they fulfill the duties and responsibilities of their servitude to Allah.

2) Those who utilize their limbs in pursuit of what they have not been created for, and dedicate them to committing sins and disobeying Allah. They are the ones whose endeavors fail and whose trade is never successful. So they deserve Allah's Punishment and Wrath and are precluded from receiving His Pleasure and Reward.

3) Those who completely suspend their limbs from engaging in any kind of productive activity; they neither serve the purpose for which they are created nor use them in obtaining the good of this worldly life, due to their ignorance and idleness. This group is even worse than the previous group, because mankind is created to worship and obey and not for incapacity. In fact, the most despised people to Allah are the useless type who are neither productive in this life nor endeavor to have a share in the Hereafter. If a person is condemned when his endeavor are dedicated for this life only, then he will without doubt be more condemned and be a greater failure when his endeavor are dedicated neither for this life nor for his Hereafter.

Parable in Three Types of People

The example of the first type is like a person who was granted a spacious land to farm and was supplied with all the instruments of need - tools, seeds and water - to help him in his work. After he prepared the land for farming, he planted all the varied types of vegetation, and he then surrounded the land with a big fence and hired guards protect it. He kept a constant watch on his farm and looked after it; fixing any spoiled parts, replacing dead plants with fresh ones, removing the harmful weeds that grew around his trees, and spending from the profit he gained from selling its harvest towards its maintenance.

The example of the second type is like a person who after he got his hands on the land, made it into a sanctuary for dangerous beasts and animals.

A land for dumping corpses and rotten bodies, and a hideout for thieves and every evil and abusive person. Even worse, he put all that he had been given to help him farm the land at the service of the evil ones dwelling in it.

He strives throughout the land to cause corruption therein and destroy crops and animals. And Allah does not like corruption. [2:205]

وَإِذَا تَوَلَّىٰ سَعَىٰ فِى ٱلْأَرْضِ لِيُفْسِدَ فِيهَا وَيُهْلِكَ ٱلْحَرْثَ وَٱلنَّسْلَ وَٱللَّهُ لَا يُحِبُّ ٱلْفَسَادَ ﴿٢٠٥﴾

The example of the third type is like a person who neglected the land and wasted the water in the desert but became regretful afterward. These examples represent the three types of people: those who are mindful and thoughtful, the people of treachery, and the heedless.

The mindful ones are always prepared and ready to fulfill the purpose for which they are created unlike the treacherous ones who betray the trust placed in them and the people of negligence and heedlessness. The affairs of righteous people, be it in their repose or activity, upon taking a bite of food or a sip of drink, in their words or silences, in a state of sleep or awakening - is always earning them reward and counted in their favour.

And their worship and remembrance of Allah draws them nearer to Allah. In contrast, the actions of the people of heedlessness are recorded against them and bring them nothing but failure and loss, not to mention distancing them from Allah. And the actions of those who betrayed the trust are performed while they are being engulfed by their inadvertency and dominated by their idleness and recklessness.

And all have degrees according to what they do; and your Lord is not heedless of what they do. *[6:132]*

وَلِكُلٍّ دَرَجَٰتٌ مِّمَّا عَمِلُوا۟ وَمَا رَبُّكَ بِغَٰفِلٍ عَمَّا يَعْمَلُونَ ۞

The grace surrounding the first group is a natural result of their obedience and acts of worship while the misery of the second group is a natural result of their transgression and treachery because Allah did not grant them all that they have in order that they use it in disobeying Him - which is a betrayal of the trust assigned to them by Allah. And, the heedlessness of the third group is a result of their being unmindful, and driven by their base-desires, therefore their failure and loss are notable as they waste their life-time serving their own pleasures and overlooking the best of all trades (i.e. trading with Allah).

The wisdom behind Allah calling His believing slaves to the ritual of Salah five times a day is to manifest His Mercy upon them; hence he has facilitated for them within it a diverse abundance of actions and rites of worship so that His believing slaves may enjoy the reward of every word, action, silence and movement practiced therein. *Upon those are the prayers from their Lord, and mercy; and those are they (who) are the right-guided. [2:157]*

$$\text{أُولَٰئِكَ عَلَيْهِمْ صَلَوَاتٌ مِّن رَّبِّهِمْ وَرَحْمَةٌ ۖ وَأُولَٰئِكَ هُمُ ٱلْمُهْتَدُونَ ﴿١٥٧﴾}$$

He is The One Who responds to your prayers, and His Angels (respond) (By Allah's command) to bring you out of the darkness into the light. [33:43]

$$\text{هُوَ ٱلَّذِي يُصَلِّي عَلَيْكُمْ وَمَلَٰئِكَتُهُ لِيُخْرِجَكُم مِّنَ ٱلظُّلُمَٰتِ إِلَى ٱلنُّورِ ۚ وَكَانَ بِٱلْمُؤْمِنِينَ رَحِيمًا ﴿٤٣﴾}$$

The Secret and Essence of Salah

The secret and essence of Salah lies in the inclination of the heart towards Allah alone and focusing attention on Him while praying. Consider the case of a person whose heart is engaged in one's own thoughts and worldly affairs; he is like a person who visits the King intending to apologize for his own mistakes and shortcomings, beseeching rain from the clouds of His Generosity and Mercy to nourish his heart enough so it can be at His service. However as soon as he arrives at His doorstep and is on the verge of calling upon Him, he turns away from the King and instead starts to busy himself with things that are most disliked and disparaged by the King. Even as his heart is inclined toward trivial matters, he still sends forth his servants (i.e. limbs) to serve Him on his behalf and to excuse and compensate for the absence of his heart.

But despite that, the Generosity and the Benevolence of the King refuse to dismiss the servants of his slaves without granting their master (i.e. slave of Allah) a portion of His Mercy.

But there is a big difference between the ones who wins and earns the trophy and those given a consolation prize out of Compassion and Mercy - Allah said: *And for all there are degrees [of reward and punishment] for what they have done, and [it is] so that He may fully compensate them for their deeds, and they will not be wronged. [46:19]*

وَلِكُلٍّ دَرَجَٰتٌ مِّمَّا عَمِلُوا۟ وَلِيُوَفِّيَهُمْ أَعْمَٰلَهُمْ وَهُمْ لَا يُظْلَمُونَ ﴿١٩﴾

Allah Created mankind solely to worship Him, and He created everything else to be at mankind's service. It is related in a Hadith qudsi that Allah said:

"O son of Adam, I created you to worship Me and created everything else for you. So, by My rights upon you, do not indulge in matters other than what I created you for."

In another narration: *"O son of Adam, I created you to worship Me, so do not play (i.e. do not be involved in idle pleasures); I guaranteed your provision in this life so do not tire yourself (i.e. seek your provision but do not make it a concern because provisions are already decreed). O son of Adam, whenever you seek Me, you shall find Me. And, whenever you find Me, you shall find everything. But, if you were to lose Me, you would lose everything. Verily, I ought to be the most beloved One to your heart."*

This is why Allah, Most High, made the Salah the means through which people can be near Him, invoke Him, earn His love and enjoy His Company.

The detachment from Allah during the intervals between the daily prayers

The 'abd of Allah experiences many times of heedlessness, detachment from Allah, and hardening of the heart, disregarding mistakes, and disposes towards sinning during the intervals between .the five daily prayers. This deplorable change takes him away from his Lord and prevents him from being near to Him and alienates him from his position as the (true) 'abd of Allah.

Even worse, he may willingly deliver himself to his enemy (i.e. Satan) who captures him, puts him in chains and locks him in the prison of his base-desires, causing him to experience nothing but anxiety, grief, sorrow and regret while being unaware of the reason behind his wretched condition.

It is through the Mercy of his Lord, the Most Compassionate, who decreed upon him a comprehensive act of worship made up of diverse phases and formats; each phase and format corresponds to the different actions he committed and conditions he experienced outside the Salah. More so, it is designed so that the goodness and benefit he acquires from each phase is in a measure proportionate to his needs, as this act of worship is prescribed to demonstrate his servitude to Allah. *Indeed, those who fear their Lord unseen will have forgiveness and great reward. [67:12]*

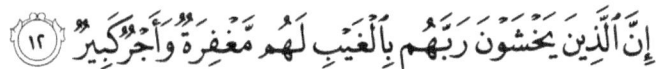

Discussion on Wudu

Wudu is the prescribed ritual whereby dirt and filth are cleansed and removed so Allah's believing slave may stand pure in His presence.

The effect of Wudu that manifests itself outwardly is the cleansing of the body and the limbs used in the act of worship (i.e. Salah). The inward effect on the other hand, is subtle, as it has to do with the purification of the heart from its sins through repentance. The two aspects of wudu are inscribed in the statement of Allah, Most High: *"Indeed, Allah loves those who are constantly repentant and loves those who purify themselves."* [2:222]

وَيَسْـَٔلُونَكَ عَنِ ٱلْمَحِيضِ قُلْ هُوَ أَذًى فَٱعْتَزِلُوا۟ ٱلنِّسَآءَ فِى ٱلْمَحِيضِ وَلَا تَقْرَبُوهُنَّ حَتَّىٰ يَطْهُرْنَ فَإِذَا تَطَهَّرْنَ فَأْتُوهُنَّ مِنْ حَيْثُ أَمَرَكُمُ ٱللَّهُ إِنَّ ٱللَّهَ يُحِبُّ ٱلتَّوَّٰبِينَ وَيُحِبُّ ٱلْمُتَطَهِّرِينَ ﴿٢٢٢﴾

Wherein He links repentance with purity, and the statement of the Prophet, peace and blessings be upon him: "O Allah, make me among those who turn to You in repentance and make me among those who are purified."

And your clothing purify. [74:4]

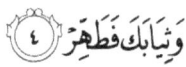

Wherein he prescribed for us to supplicate to be among the cleansed and among the repentant ones. Allah therefore, perfected for His believing 'abd degree and layers of purity and servitude (to Him); inwardly and outwardly at every stratum; bearing witness that there is no ilāh worthy of worship except Allah and that the Prophets, is His Messenger purifies him from disbelief and polytheism, turning to Him in repentance purifies him from sins, and using water in wudu purifies him from visible filth.

Perfecting one's servitude in attending the Mosque

In particular Allah prescribed that His 'abd be in the most perfect level of purity (i.e. wudu) prior to entering upon Him and standing before Him (i.e. in Salah) as only then does He, Exalted be He, grant permission for His 'abd to stand in His presence - after he has become pure both from the outside and the inside, thus signifying that he is not a rebellious 'abd. And when he enters His house (i.e. masjid), the place where he evinces his servitude to Allah, he becomes one of His slaves. This explains the reason why attending the masjid to pray the compulsory Salah in congregation -which some scholars consider obligatory to do and others consider highly commendable to do - is deemed from the aspects of perfection of one's servitude to Allah. The example of a heedless person is like a rebellious 'abd disobeying his master; he ceases to put his limbs and heart at the service of his Master, which is the sole purpose for which he is created.

But, as soon as he comes back to his master, he effectively nullifies his state of disobedience and restores his state of obedience. And when he stands before Him in humility and submission (in Salah), the Compassion and Kindness of his Master over- whelms and engulfs him and accepts him after having rejected him before.

Servitude in al-Takbir

The 'abd of Allah is then ordered to stand with his face in the direction of the Qiblah all the while having his heart facing Him as well (being fully attentive to Him) so as to renounce his previous state of rebellion and to stop turning away (from his Lord). The slave (of Allah) should therefore stand up before his Master in humility and submission calling for His Compassion with his hands thrown at his sides and his head low, while at the same time his heart is fully attentive to Him in a state of humility, as he devotes all his senses to His service and glorification by declaring with his tongue and proclaiming in his heart that He is the Greatest, which is to express that Allah is greater than anything he may have in his heart. And he affirms this statement by dismissing everything except Allah from his heart so his heart is completely occupied with Allah and nothing else. This is because occupying himself with anything else would connote that he finds what he is busy with is of more importance or greater than Allah. Indeed, a person whose heart is busied with what distracts him from Allah (in Salah) is someone whose heart does not conform to the statement made by his tongue declaring Allah is the Greatest. Having the heart in harmony with the tongue when saying that Allah is the Greatest will strip the heart from the attire of arrogance as such garment does not befit the state of his enslavement to Allah. Furthermore, it would prevent the heart from thinking of anything except Allah. This is because the rights of these two words; Allah is Greater than everything (Allah Akbar), and the resolve to establish his servitude to Allah through the takbir protects the heart from the aforementioned defects (being occupied with something else other than Allah and wearing a garment that does not befit the servitude to Allah).

Servitude in al-Istiftah

[The Opening Supplication]

And when he says:

سُبْحَانَكَ اللَّهُمَّ وَبِحَمْدِكَ وَتَبَارَكَ اسْمُكَ

Glory and praise be to You, O Allah. Blessed be Your name

وَتَعَالَى جَدُّكَ وَلاَ إِلَهَ غَيْرُكَ

and exalted be Your majesty,
there is none worthy of worship except You

And then glorifies Him and praises Him in repetition with what befits Him, he comes out of the state of heedlessness that stands as a barrier between him and Allah. Then, he greets and praises with expressions that befit His Kingship when someone enters upon Him, to glorify Him and as a prelude to his own needs and requests that he hopes the King to grant. This is why praising over and over again is considered from the etiquettes of expressing one's servitude to Allah and glorifying Him, and the means whereby the 'abd receives the attention of Allah as well as His pleasure and approval to fulfill his requests.

As he is about to recite the Quran, he precedes it by seeking refuge in Allah from the accursed Satan who never spares any effort in his tireless endeavor, to bring about the downfall of the 'abd of Allah -

especially when the 'abd is in a station of utmost honor (i.e. Salah) while seeking to perform the single most beneficial deed for this life and the Hereafter. Hence, he (Satan) is fervently determined to prevent the 'abd of Allah from praying by any means; failing to do so he wants to see to it that at the very least, his heart does not benefit from it (i.e. the Salah) by casting into his heart all sorts of whispers and thoughts to distract it from fulfilling the duties of servitude to Allah. Therefore Allah has ordered His slave to take refuge in Him from Satan (before starting his recitation in Salah) to assure the safety of his Salah, so that his heart may be revived and illuminated by the understanding he acquires from contemplating the words of Allah as He is the Master in whose hand is the success, grace and life of his heart. This also explains why Satan is keen to distract his heart from understanding the words of Quran when recited.

It is from Allah's knowledge about the enmity and resentment of Satan against His believing slaves and their incapacity to face him that he ordained upon them to take refuge in Him from Satan so that He may suffice them against his evil and harm. It is as if He is saying to His slaves, you cannot win against this enemy; thus take refuge in Me and I shall protect you from him and safeguard you from his evil and harm.

Ibn Taymiyyah's advice to Ibn Qayyim

Shaykh al-Islam, Ibn Taymmiyah, may Allah honour his soul and illuminate his grave, once said to me (explaining with a metaphorical example the purpose of seeking refuge in Allah from Satan): "If the shepherd's dog ever barks at you attempting to attack you, then do not engage it in a fight.

Instead, turn to the shepherd and seek his help for he will leash it and save you the trouble." When a person takes refuge in Allah from the accursed Satan, He protects him and keeps away Satan's harm and evil from reaching him. *And if an evil suggestion comes to you from Satan, then seek refuge in Allah. Indeed, He is Hearing and Knowing. [7:200]*

وَإِمَّا يَنزَغَنَّكَ مِنَ ٱلشَّيْطَٰنِ نَزْغٌ فَٱسْتَعِذْ بِٱللَّهِ ۚ إِنَّهُۥ سَمِيعٌ عَلِيمٌ ﴿٢٠٠﴾

And when thou recites the Quran, seek refuge in Allah from Satan the outcast. [16:98]

فَإِذَا قَرَأْتَ ٱلْقُرْءَانَ فَٱسْتَعِذْ بِٱللَّهِ مِنَ ٱلشَّيْطَٰنِ ٱلرَّجِيمِ ﴿٩٨﴾

Take time each day to explore the meanings of the Quran and witness its fascinating, awe-inspiring wonders. Collect from its treasures and gems that no eyes have ever seen, no ears have ever heard, and no mind has ever conceived.

It is only his base desires and Satan that stand as a barrier between you and all these wonders, because his base desires always incline towards the whispers and temptations of Satan. However, as soon as you distance yourself from Satan and manages to expel him from your heart, the King takes over charge of your heart, holding it fast to the truth and reminding it of that which will assure its safety and everlasting happiness. As the 'abd of Allah starts to recite the Quran, he effectively begins addressing his Lord and invoking Him. Therefore, he should beware of invoking Him while his heart is busy with something else, as this shall make him deserving of His Contempt and Anger; he will be like a man upon whom a king bestowed his favour and then granted him the permission to speak before him, but as the man started to speak to the king he turned his back towards the king, turning his face away from him, which made the king angry and furious. And if this is the case among mankind, then the contempt and Anger of the King, the Lord of all Worlds, the Sustainer of Heavens and Earth, shall be beyond imagination.

The State of the 'abd in al-Fatihah

A person should pause a little at the end of each ayah he recites from al-Fatihah to wait for the response from his Lord; as if he is waiting to hear Him to say" "My 'abd has praised Me" when he recites: "*All Praises and thanks are due to Allah, the Lord of the worlds." [1:2]*

And "My 'abd has extolled Me," after reciting;

The Entirely Merciful, the Especially Merciful. [1:3]

ٱلرَّحْمَٰنِ ٱلرَّحِيمِ ۝

And "My 'abd has glorified Me," after reciting;

Sovereign of the Day of Recompense. [1:4]

مَٰلِكِ يَوْمِ ٱلدِّينِ ۝

And "This is between Me and My 'abd shall have what he requested," after reciting; *It is You we worship and You we ask for help. [1:5]*

إِيَّاكَ نَعْبُدُ وَإِيَّاكَ نَسْتَعِينُ ۝

Only the one who has experienced the true taste and sweetness of Salah can realize that no other statement could ever replace the takbir and al-Fatihah in Salah, just as how no acts can ever replace the standing, bowing down, and prostration in Salah.

This is because each act and each statement in Salah has a unique effect and comprises a distinctive experience, besides its representation of the person's servitude to Allah.

The statement of Allah: *"All Praises and thanks are due to Allah, the Lord of the worlds."* [1:2]

confirms the perfection of Allah's Names and Attributes, and declares His transcendence above every defect and shortcoming, be it in respect to His Names, Attributes or Actions. All His Actions comprise Wisdom, Mercy, Justice and Benefit, and all His Attributes are Perfect and Lauded, and all His Names are Supreme and Beautiful.

The meanings of Al-hamd

The praise entitled to Him fills up this worldly life and the Hereafter as does the heavens and earth and all that is between them and contained within them. The entire universe utters His Praise.

The creation, its affairs, existence and non-existence as well as its sustainability owe themselves to His Praiseworthiness. Truly, everything exists just to praise Him for it is the objective and purpose of every creature. Every object in existence attests to the praise that He is entitled to; the Messengers He sent and the Books He sent down entail that He be praised; the creation of Paradise and Hell calls for praising Him. Paradise inhabited with its people and Hell inhabited with its people testify to the praise He is entitled for.

The obedience and disobedience of mankind have not transpired except to testify to the praise Allah is worthy of. The leaves of trees would not fall nor would atoms move, had it not been for His praise. Exalted be He, is praised for His Essence even if none of His slaves had ever praised Him, just as He is the One and Only llāh even if none of His slaves had been monotheists - and He is the true llāh worthy of worship even if none of His slaves had believed in Him. He praised Himself through the tongue of His Prophet; as the Messenger of Allah, peace and blessings be upon him, said: "Allah said on the tongue of His Prophet: *"Allah Hears the one who praises Him."*

Keeping this in perspective it is evident that it is actually He who praises Himself on the tongue of His slaves, because when a person praises Him it is only due to His permission that such praise is uttered by their tongues, and is established in their heart through his permission. Truly, to Him is all the praise and to Him belongs everything; in His Hand lies all goodness; He is the absolute controller of everything, all that is apparent or hidden. This is only a brief glimpse of the countless aspects of servitude to Allah included in this statement al-hamd, it is only a drop of water out of the ocean of the knowledge of what servitude to Allah comprises and entails. From among the implications of being a true 'abd to Allah is to realize that the act of praising Him for a bounty that He bestowed upon you is itself worthy of praising Him again for it (i.e. praising Him) necessitates praising Him (again) for facilitating His praise on the tongue of His 'abd perpetually. In reality, if a person were to devote every single one of his breaths towards praising his Lord for even a single bounty of His numerous blessings that He bestowed upon him, it would not be enough - this is because no one is capable of praising Him enough. And even if he does not praise Him for any of His graces upon him, he should praise Him for preventing harm from him (at least). Furthermore, he should praise Him for guiding him to praise Him. Al-Awza'i said: I heard someone say: "All praise is due to Allah; if not for a grace He bestowed, it is for a harm He prevented."

Another aspect of servitude to Allah in "al-hamd" is that it connotes an acknowledgment that were it not for Allah's guidance that inspired and enabled the 'abd of Allah to praise Him, he would be incapable of praising Him. He is therefore praised for it because He inspired his tongue and heart to praise Him; indeed no one would be guided if Allah did not permit it. From the other aspects of servitude to Allah found in "al-hamd" is that it encompasses even the minutiae of the circumstances and state of affairs of the 'abd of Allah; the hidden and the known, the loved and the despised. It even covers the details of the circumstances and conditions of mankind in its entirety; the righteous and the evil ones, the dignified ones and the abased ones. In reality He is to be praised for all of that, even if His slaves are unable to comprehend the wisdom behind it or realize the magnitude of praise He deserves for all of that. To praise Allah is a manifestation of guidance that Allah inspires in His slaves; some indulge in praising Him abundantly whereas there are others whose share is minimal, dependent on the level of knowledge one has about his Lord. The Prophet, peace and blessings be upon him, said: "And then He will inspire me to praise Him with such praises as I do not know (now), I will praise Him with those praises and will fall down, prostrating before Him."

Servitude in "Lord of all the worlds"

Reciting the statement: *"All praise is due to Allah, Lord of the worlds." [1:2]*

Wherein the servitude to Allah manifests itself through the acknowledgment of the 'abd of Allah of the singularity and exclusivity of Allah's Lordship. And just as He is the Lord of the worlds, their Creator, the One who gives them livelihood and manages their affairs, and the One who suffices them, He is also their only Ilāh that they worship exclusively, take refuge in and turn to in times of need and hardship - for indeed He is the only Lord and the only Ilāh worthy of worship.

Servitude in "The Merciful (al-Rahmān), the Most Merciful (al-Rahim)"

The statement of Allah:

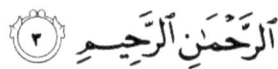

The Entirely Merciful, the Especially Merciful. comprises an aspect of servitude to Allah that is exclusive to Him; when the 'abd of Allah recites it, he testifies to the All-encompassing Mercy of Allah that covers everything and embraces every being; every creature enjoys a share of His Mercy. In reality, it is by His Mercy that His 'abd stands up (in Salah) before Him; it was related in a report that Angel Jibrll, peace be upon him, say every night: "Let so- and-so get up (to pray) and let so-and-so remain asleep." It is the Mercy of Allah that puts a person at His service to invoke Him with His divine words (i.e. Quran), beseech His Mercy, Kindness and Guidance, and adjure Him to perfect His Grace upon him in this life and in the Hereafter. Indeed, His Mercy embraces all things just like how He embraces all things in His Knowledge, and His praise manifests in all things. Allah said: *"Our Lord, You have encompassed all things in mercy and knowledge, so forgive those who have repented and followed Your way and protect them from the punishment of Fire."* [40:7]

$$رَبَّنَا وَسِعْتَ كُلَّ شَيْءٍ رَحْمَةً وَعِلْمًا فَاغْفِرْ لِلَّذِينَ تَابُوا وَاتَّبَعُوا سَبِيلَكَ وَقِهِمْ عَذَابَ الْجَحِيمِ ۝$$

While, the favoured slaves bask in His Mercy, others are deprived from this Mercy as they are expelled from enjoying His exclusive Mercy (i.e. Salah).

Servitude in "Master of the Day of Judgment"

The aspect of servitude to Allah that manifests itself in:

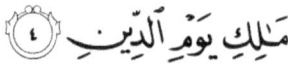

"Sovereign of the Day of Recompense." [1:4]

connotes the humility and submission of His slaves, as well as His Justice. It also calls upon the slave to abstain from being unjust to himself by avoiding sins, and to reflect upon the tenets introduced in this ayah, namely: the affirmation of the Day of Judgment, and the sole authority of questioning and judging the creation (i.e. mankind and Jinn) for all their good deeds and wrong- doings resting with Allah. All these tenets and meanings predicate His praise; Allah said:

"And you will see the angels surrounding the Throne, exalting [Allah] with praise of their Lord. And it will be judged between them in truth, and it will be said, "[All] praise to Allah, Lord of the worlds." [39:75]

وَتَرَى ٱلْمَلَٰٓئِكَةَ حَآفِّينَ مِنْ حَوْلِ ٱلْعَرْشِ يُسَبِّحُونَ بِحَمْدِ رَبِّهِمْ وَقُضِيَ بَيْنَهُم بِٱلْحَقِّ وَقِيلَ ٱلْحَمْدُ لِلَّهِ رَبِّ ٱلْعَٰلَمِينَ ﴿٧٥﴾

It is also related that the entire creation, including the people of Paradise and the people of Hell, shall praise Allah on that Day for His Justice and Grace. This is why Allah responds to the slave's reciting *"All Praises and thanks are due to Allah"* by saying: "My 'abd praised Me."

The meanings of Thanā and Tamjid

Allah is praised with His Attribute of Perfection in the first two verses: for the ayah:

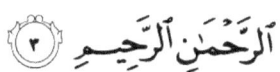

"The Entirely Merciful, the Especially Merciful" [1:3]

Reiterates His Attributes of Perfection, to which His response was "My 'abd has glorified Me"; this is because the Arabic word "thanā" refers to manifold praise that is offered to one who is worthy of being praised for his numerous commendable attributes. Therefore the statement, *"all praise is due to Him"* is considered "thanā" and the Most Compassion (to mankind), the Most Merciful (to believers)" is the attribution of the (praiseworthy) attribute of Mercy to Allah. When the ayah:

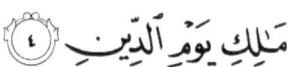

"Master of the Day of Judgement." [1:4]

is recited, the slave (of Allah) ascribes to Allah the sole owner- ship of authority on the Day of Judgment where His Justice, Pride and Glory as well as the truthfulness of His Messengers are manifested, and the reality that He is the true King to whom belong this world and Hereafter. In response to this ayah, Allah says: "'My 'abd has glorified Me" because this manner of praise is called glorification (tamjid) in that it entails praising Allah with respect to His Attributes of Greatness, Glory, Justice and Kindness.

Servitude in "You Alone we worship"

After reciting the ayah:

إِيَّاكَ نَعْبُدُ وَإِيَّاكَ نَسْتَعِينُ ۝

"You Alone we worship." [1:5]

The 'abd of Allah anticipates the response from his Lord, which is: *"This is between Me and My 'abd and My 'abd shall have what he requested."*

You ought to reflect upon the aspects of servitude to Allah that these words carry, as well as the responsibilities that come along with each one of them. And, you ought to recognize the difference between the word that has been used in respect to Allah and the word used in respect to His 'abd, and understand the reason and wisdom behind using them in such a manner. And, you ought to realize the difference between the dimension of Tawhid conveyed in "You Alone we worship", and the dimension of Tawhid contained in "You Alone we ask for help", and then understand the purpose of placing this ayah in the middle - between the preceding ayah pertaining to the praise of Allah and the succeeding ayah that comprise a supplication made by the 'abd to Allah, and to understand the wisdom behind placing the part "You Alone we worship" before "You Alone we ask for help", as well as the wisdom behind having the part "You Alone" precede the word "we worship", and the part "You Alone" precede the phrase "We ask for help."

The wisdom behind al-Isti'ānah

I say: The wisdom behind having the part "You Alone we worship" precede the part "You Alone we ask for help" is that the worship is intended for Allah while the help is intended for the 'abd. Allah is the One to be worshipped and He is the One from whom help is to be sought.

The part "You Alone worship" is so the 'abd declares that he devotes to Him all his worship, including good deeds performed with sincerity meaning that they are intended for His sake only, and the beneficial knowledge that the person acquires by which he comes to know and love Him sincerely and truthfully.

To be worshipped is Allah's right upon His 'abd and seeking His Help includes asking His assistance in all his affairs. Every act of worship that is not facilitated by Allah and which is not intended sincerely and truthfully for His sake alone shall be rendered null and void. And any attempt of asking help from anyone other than Allah shall lead to nothing but humiliation and failure.

You should contemplate all the beneficial knowledge derived from this ayah, which shall safeguard, protect and maintain the pristine state of a slave's servitude to Allah, the Creator of Everything, from all deficiencies and harm. It is an evident demonstration of pure and true servitude to Allah.

You also need to reflect upon how the entire message of the Quran revolves around the meanings contained in this ayah, and not only that but also the purpose behind creation, the essence of religious commandments and prohibitions, of divine reward and retribution, and of this worldly life and the Hereafter. And reflect upon how these verses mention the greatest of all objectives (i.e. worship) and the most perfect of all means (seeking His Help), and the compelling usage of the second-person narrative "You" instead of the third-person pronoun "Him". Actually an entire volume could be dedicated to this particular topic as it were, but I do not wish to divert from the main theme of this chapter, other- wise I would have elaborated on it further.

The Need of the 'abd for "Guide us to the Straight Path"

The 'abd of Allah should reflect deeply upon how the ayah, *"Guide us to the Straight Path."[1:6]*

Expresses his perpetual needs through the various meanings it comprises namely;

1) Knowing the truth
2) The way to it
3) Acting upon it
4) Holding fast to it, and
5) Calling for it and forbearing harm caused to you by those whom you call

Yet being in a state of perfect guidance cannot be realized unless the 'abd of Allah is able to receive complete guidance. Thus, whenever he falls short in some aspects pertaining to his ability to assimilate guidance, the state of his enlightenment will be affected accordingly. This is because the 'abd of Allah is in need of this guidance, both inwardly and outwardly, and in all his affairs.

Divisions of guidance that the 'abd is in need of

The following are types of guidance that the 'abd is in need of:

1) Guidance to repent from all his wrongdoings, from deviated knowledge and insincere intentions. Hence, as the slave is in constant need to repent, he is always in need of this type of guidance.

2) Guidance to be acquainted with the finer details of the beliefs and actions that he has, in a broad sense, already been guided to.

3) Guidance to matters he requires in order to further perfect and increase his guidance.

4) To have guidance in matters that he needs in the future, just as he needed in the past.

5) Guidance to have sound beliefs in matters in which he lacks any belief

6) Guidance to have sound beliefs in matters he has based upon wrong and deviated beliefs.

This form of guidance abrogates his deviated beliefs and replaces them with the right and sound ones.

7) Guidance to have the will and desire in matters that he possesses the capability to do and that he ought to do, but for which he does not yet have the desire to carry out.

8) Guidance to have the desire as well as the capability to do things that he ought to but that he neither desires nor is capable of.

9) Guidance to maintain and preserve the sound beliefs, knowledge and good deeds that he already possesses.

Indeed, asking for guidance is the greatest among all his needs and the most crucial of all his requests. For this reason, Allah enacted that His slaves beseech Him for His guidance several times on a daily basis when he is in his best state, during the five obligatory prayers (i.e. Salah) because all this manifests the dire need of the slave to attain this guidance and how significantly important it is to him.

Additionally, Allah clarifies that the path of those who are truly guided is different from the path of those who earned His anger (the Jews) and those who are astray (the Christians and others). From that perspective, mankind is divided into three types with respect to guidance:

1) Those whom Allah favored with His guidance and preserved it for them. However, the individual share of the ones in this category depends on how much guidance each one of them has received.

2) Those who are astray because they have neither received guidance nor were prepared for it.

3) Those with whom Allah is Angry because they recognized the truth but did not follow it.

The ones who are astray deviate from the truth because (in their quest for the truth) they become lost and bewildered and thus unable to find the right path, leading them to totally sever them- selves from the truth and the knowledge leading to it. As for those who earned Allah's Wrath, they are the ones who despite knowing the truth still deviated from it, and as a consequence never benefited from their knowledge because they refrained from acting upon the truth they knew. On the other hand, those whom Allah favoured with guidance stand apart by virtue of their guidance, knowledge, beliefs and deeds. And, Allah is the Facilitator of Success and Guide to the truth.

Servitude in raising the hands

As the slave is about to bow down, it has been prescribed upon him to raise his hands as a show of his deference to the

Command of Allah and to manifest the servitude of his hands to Allah, in adherence to the way of the Prophet, peace and blessings be upon him, and as a gesture that beautifies the Salah. It is indeed the adornment of Salah and the expression of one's glorification to its parts.

Allah has then instructed that he pronounce the keyword of Salah; that is to say takbir, which he must do every time he intends to move from one pillar (of Salah) to another, as He has instructed the slogan of hajj; that is to say the talbiyah when the pilgrim moves from one act of hajj to another. All this so His 'abd knows that the secret of Salah lies in extolling and glorifying Allah through worshipping Him alone.

The next act of bowing down is prescribed wherein the 'abd visibly demonstrates his submission before the Greatness of his Lord and shows humility before the Pride and Glory of his Lord.

Servitude in al-Ruku'

The praise of Allah in this pillar is to bow his back down, lowering his head while his tongue utters the words: "Glory be to my Lord, the Greatest." Through this act, his heart, body and tongue submit to Allah in a most sublime manner that brings together the feeling of humility, humbleness, Allah's glorification, and His remembrance, uniquely distinguishes his submission to Allah from the submission of the slaves (i.e. people) to one another. This is because submission is the attribute of slaves and Glory is the attribute of the Lord.

The perfect state of servitude that manifests while bowing down is when the slave dismisses his ego, accepts his status as a slave of Allah, and empties his heart from any glorification he might have had about anyone besides Allah and replaces all that with his glorification of Allah as the only Ilāh worthy of worship.

When the heart is overwhelmed by his glorification of His Lord, his glorification of himself or of any other created being will be dismissed from his heart.

Notwithstanding the outward physical movement of the body when bowing down, this pillar is in reality an act of worship that is foremost prescribed to be performed by the heart; the physical movement of the body is a mere accessory to complete the pillar.

Servitude in Al-Qiyām

As the 'abd rises from the bowing position to stand upright once more, returning his body to its most fitting posture, it is prescribed that the 'abd exalt Allah to thank Him and praise Him for His bounties and for facilitating him and guiding him to experience this humility and submission that He prevented others from experiencing. Just as the Qur'an is prescribed for the 'abd to recite while he was in the standing posture before bowing, Allah prescribed for His slave to praise Him and glorify Him when he is standing erect after having risen from bowing. In fact, the effect of this pillar on the heart is unique; an effect that cannot be produced by anything except the act of the bowing that preceded it.

It is an essential pillar similar to the other pillars of Salah such as bowing down and prostration. And for this reason the Messenger of Allah, peace and blessings be upon him, used to prolong this standing (after the bowing down) just as he pro- longed the pillars of bowing and prostration, and he used to praise, glorify and extol Allah much therein, and exalt Him as I have mentioned before when I explained the description of his Salah. He used to say in his night prayers: *"To my Lord be all praise, to my Lord be all praise."* repeating it until his standing was as along as his ruku.

Servitude in Al-Sugud

The 'abd is subsequently prescribed to say: "Allah is the Most Great," and then to fall down in prostration to the floor to let all his limbs individually demonstrate their servitude to Allah.

His forehead placed on the floor before his Lord, his face - the most honorable part of his body - comes together with the dust on the floor, and all the while his heart humbles itself to Allah.

The arrangement of this posture is such that his lower body ends up in a higher level than his upper limbs (i.e. the face), emphasizing his submission. His heart and body are thus rendered humble and submissive before the Greatness and Glory of the Lord. Moreover, when the state of the heart conforms to the state of the body in this position (i.e. both are humble, submissive and down to earth), it is as if the heart too prostrates to Allah along with the forehead, nose, face, hands, knees and feet. An 'abd with such humility and submissiveness shall be among Allah's favoured servants.

This is because the closest an 'abd comes to his Lord is when he is in the state of prostration. In this posture, it is prescribed for the 'abd to not have any part of his body depend on any other part for support; that is, he should avoid placing the weight of his thighs on his legs, maintain a space between his belly and his legs, and keep a space between his arms by spreading them to the sides away from his body.

This is so that each part of his physical self can individually demonstrate its slavery to Allah. And it follows from what has been said that the slave (of Allah) should in this posture be at the closest point to his Lord, as the Prophet, peace and blessings be upon him, said: "The closest an 'abd is to his Lord is when he is prostrating."

The reality of the prostration of the heart is its submission to Allah, and the heart is able to remain in prostration until the Day of Judgment. One of the righteous Salaf was asked: "Does the heart prostrate?" He answered: Indeed it does, by Allah it prostrates such that it does not raise its head even once, and remains in prostration until it meets Allah, Exalted be He.

The Salah is built upon five pillars

This points to the worship, humility and submissiveness of the heart to its Lord as a perpetual condition wherever it may be: in constant regard for Allah, whether in solitude or in the company of others. As-Salah is built upon five pillars; recitation (qira'a), standing (qiyam), bowing down (ruku), prostration (sujud) and remembrance of Allah (dhiker).

It is tacitly called after these actions i.e. it is called qiyam based on the ayah: *"Arise [to pray] the night, except for a little."* [73:2]

قُمِ ٱلَّيۡلَ إِلَّا قَلِيلًا ۝

"Maintain with care the [obligatory] prayers and [in particular] the middle prayer and stand before Allah, devoutly obedient." [2:238]

حَٰفِظُوا۟ عَلَى ٱلصَّلَوَٰتِ وَٱلصَّلَوٰةِ ٱلۡوُسۡطَىٰ وَقُومُوا۟ لِلَّهِ قَٰنِتِينَ ۝

Establish prayer at the decline of the sun [from its meridian] until the darkness of the night and [also] the Qur'an of dawn. Indeed, the recitation of dawn is ever witnessed. [17:78]

أَقِمِ ٱلصَّلَوٰةَ لِدُلُوكِ ٱلشَّمۡسِ إِلَىٰ غَسَقِ ٱلَّيۡلِ وَقُرۡءَانَ ٱلۡفَجۡرِ إِنَّ قُرۡءَانَ ٱلۡفَجۡرِ كَانَ مَشۡهُودًا ۝

Indeed, your Lord knows, [O Muḥammad], that you stand [in prayer] almost two thirds of the night or half of it or a third of it, and [so do] a group of those with you. And Allah determines [the extent of] the night and the day.

He has known that you [Muslims] will not be able to do it and has turned to you in forgiveness, so recite what is easy [for you] of the Qur'an. He has known that there will be among you those who are ill and others traveling throughout the land seeking [something] of the bounty of Allah and others fighting for the cause of Allah. So recite what is easy from it and establish prayer and give zakah and loan Allah a goodly loan. And whatever good you put forward for yourselves - you will find it with Allah. It is better and greater in reward. And seek forgiveness of Allah. Indeed, Allah is Forgiving and Merciful. [73:20]

۞ إِنَّ رَبَّكَ يَعْلَمُ أَنَّكَ تَقُومُ أَدْنَىٰ مِن ثُلُثَيِ ٱلَّيْلِ وَنِصْفَهُۥ وَثُلُثَهُۥ وَطَآئِفَةٌ مِّنَ ٱلَّذِينَ مَعَكَ ۚ وَٱللَّهُ يُقَدِّرُ ٱلَّيْلَ وَٱلنَّهَارَ ۚ عَلِمَ أَن لَّن تُحْصُوهُ فَتَابَ عَلَيْكُمْ ۖ فَٱقْرَءُوا۟ مَا تَيَسَّرَ مِنَ ٱلْقُرْءَانِ ۚ عَلِمَ أَن سَيَكُونُ مِنكُم مَّرْضَىٰ ۙ وَءَاخَرُونَ يَضْرِبُونَ فِى ٱلْأَرْضِ يَبْتَغُونَ مِن فَضْلِ ٱللَّهِ ۙ وَءَاخَرُونَ يُقَٰتِلُونَ فِى سَبِيلِ ٱللَّهِ ۖ فَٱقْرَءُوا۟ مَا تَيَسَّرَ مِنْهُ ۚ وَأَقِيمُوا۟ ٱلصَّلَوٰةَ وَءَاتُوا۟ ٱلزَّكَوٰةَ وَأَقْرِضُوا۟ ٱللَّهَ قَرْضًا حَسَنًا ۚ وَمَا تُقَدِّمُوا۟ لِأَنفُسِكُم مِّنْ خَيْرٍ تَجِدُوهُ عِندَ ٱللَّهِ هُوَ خَيْرًا وَأَعْظَمَ أَجْرًا ۚ وَٱسْتَغْفِرُوا۟ ٱللَّهَ ۖ إِنَّ ٱللَّهَ غَفُورٌ رَّحِيمٌۢ ﴿٢٠﴾

And establish prayer and give zakah and bow with those who bow [in worship and obedience]. *[2:43]*

وَأَقِيمُوا۟ ٱلصَّلَوٰةَ وَءَاتُوا۟ ٱلزَّكَوٰةَ وَٱرْكَعُوا۟ مَعَ ٱلرَّٰكِعِينَ ﴿٤٣﴾

And when it is said to them, "Bow [in prayer]," they do not bow. *[77:48]*

وَإِذَا قِيلَ لَهُمُ ٱرْكَعُوا۟ لَا يَرْكَعُونَ ﴿٤٨﴾

So exalt Allah with praise of your Lord and be of those who prostrate [to Him]. *[15:98]*

فَسَبِّحْ بِحَمْدِ رَبِّكَ وَكُن مِّنَ ٱلسَّٰجِدِينَ ﴿٩٨﴾

No! Do not obey him. But prostrate and draw near to Allah. *[96:19]*

كَلَّا لَا تُطِعْهُ وَٱسْجُدْ وَٱقْتَرِب ۩ ﴿١٩﴾

O you who have believed, when [the adhan] is called for the prayer on the day of Jumu'ah [Friday], then proceed to the remembrance of Allah and leave trade. That is better for you, if you only knew. *[62:9]*

$$\text{يَٰٓأَيُّهَا ٱلَّذِينَ ءَامَنُوٓاْ إِذَا نُودِيَ لِلصَّلَوٰةِ مِن يَوْمِ ٱلْجُمُعَةِ فَٱسْعَوْاْ إِلَىٰ ذِكْرِ ٱللَّهِ وَذَرُواْ ٱلْبَيْعَ ۚ ذَٰلِكُمْ خَيْرٌ لَّكُمْ إِن كُنتُمْ تَعْلَمُونَ ۝٩}$$

O you who have believed, let not your wealth and your children divert you from remembrance of Allah. And whoever does that - then those are the losers. [63:9]

$$\text{يَٰٓأَيُّهَا ٱلَّذِينَ ءَامَنُواْ لَا تُلْهِكُمْ أَمْوَٰلُكُمْ وَلَآ أَوْلَٰدُكُمْ عَن ذِكْرِ ٱللَّهِ ۚ وَمَن يَفْعَلْ ذَٰلِكَ فَأُوْلَٰٓئِكَ هُمُ ٱلْخَٰسِرُونَ ۝٩}$$

The most honourable action in Salah is prostration and the most honourable dhikr in Salah is the recitation of the Qur'an; the first Surah that was revealed to the Prophet, peace and blessings be upon him, was Surah al-'Alaq, whose first ayah is to: *"Read! In the Name of your Lord, Who has created (all that exists)." [96:1]*

$$\text{ٱقْرَأْ بِٱسْمِ رَبِّكَ ٱلَّذِى خَلَقَ ۝١}$$

And whose last ayah is to: *"No! Do not obey him. But prostrate and draw near to Allah."* *[96:19]*

كَلَّا لَا تُطِعْهُ وَٱسْجُدْ وَٱقْتَرِب ۩ ﴿١٩﴾

Thus, the structure of the unit (ruk'ah) in Salah is composed accordingly; it starts with recitation and ends in prostration.

The State of the 'abd between the Two Prostrations

Next it is prescribed for the 'abd (of Allah) to rise from his prostration to assume the sitting pose until his limbs enter a state of repose. Given that this pillar has been placed in the middle of two prostrations earns it great significance. The Messenger of Allah, peace and blessings be upon him, used to spend about the same amount of time in this pillar as he did during prostration, and during it he used to invoke and beseech

Allah for His Forgiveness, Mercy, Guidance and Provision. The experience and effect of this pillar is unique and different from the pillar of prostration: in this posture the slave kneels down before his Lord apologizing for all the sins he committed and hoping for His Forgiveness and Mercy, and asking Him to help him against his own self that incites him to commit acts of wrongdoing. The Prophet, peace be upon him, used to ask for much forgiveness from Allah in this position. He used to say: "*O my Lord, forgive me, O my Lord, forgive me, O my Lord, forgive me.*"

O worshipper, be in the Salah like a man who agreed to guarantee the debt of a person who turned out to be deceitful and kept delaying the payment of his debt. And because you are the guarantor of this man you will be called to pay the debt in place of him, so you call for every form of available help to force this man to pay his debt in order to release yourself from this commitment. The heart is in partnership with the *nafs* (inner self) in evil and good, punishment and reward, praise and condemnation. The *nafs* is fundamentally rebellious in nature, always seeking to break out of its condition of slavery to Allah and inclined to ignore the rights of Allah as well as the rights of mankind. Nevertheless, the heart follows and submits to the *nafs* whenever it is dominant and strong, and conversely the *nafs* follows and submits to the heart whenever the latter is dominant and strong.

The Wisdom behind the Second Prostration

It is therefore prescribed for the 'abd to sit down in the presence of Allah with humility, admitting his mistakes and repenting from sins, hoping for His Mercy and asking for His Forgiveness, Guidance, Provision and Protection. These five things that the 'abd beseeches His Lord for include the good of this life as well as the good of the Hereafter. This is because the 'abd of Allah is in dire need of protecting himself against all harm, as well as attaining what benefits him in this life and the Hereafter. His share of Allah's provision covers the provision intended for his body, heart and soul, and Allah is the best Provider. Protection and safety keep away the harm, guidance brings forth the benefits of the hereafter, forgiveness protects him from harm both in this life and the Hereafter.

Mercy covers all the aforementioned and guidance covers its details. Then it is prescribed for the 'abd to fall in prostration once more, because one prostration is not enough as the case was with bowing down. This is due to the virtue and honour of prostration, not to mention it being the position in which the 'abd is closest to his Lord. It also takes into account that prostration is more prominently recognized as a mark of servitude compared to the other actions of Salah. Thus it is the culmination of the rak'ah in relation to which the preceding actions serve as a preamble that lead up to it. From this point of view it is like the tawaf of ziyarah (the tawaf of visit): just as how the closest an 'abd comes to his Lord in Salah is during tawaf, likewise the closest an 'abd comes to his Lord in Salah is in prostration.

It is reported that the man who asked for the hand of Abdullah Ibn Umar's (RA) daughter called out to him while he was circulating around the Ka'bah but Abdullah Ibn 'Umar (RA) did not reply to him. After he finished his tawaf, he said to the man: "How can you think of a matter related to this worldly life when we are standing in the Sight of Allah in tawaf! It would appear that the reason Allah made the action of bowing down to precede prostration is that the slave should move gradually from one act to another that is higher than the preceding one in rank.

The wisdom behind prescribing the actions and the statements of Salah to be performed several times in succession during Salah is because they are the sustenance of the heart and the soul without which they cannot survive.

It is like the example of man whose hunger and thirst cannot be quelled by a single morsel of food or a single sip of drink, unless he eats or drinks more and more until he reaches the point of satiation. Eating one bite can never satisfy the hunger of a person; in fact, it may make him even hungrier. One of the righteous Salaf said: "The example of the man who prays without achieving calmness and tranquility in his Salah is like a person who is hungry, but when food is served he takes only one or two handfuls! What then will it do for him!?"

Performing each pillar and reciting each statement multiple times intensifies the perception of servitude and nearness to Allah, as performing them a second time is an expression of one's gratitude to Allah for guiding him to do these acts the first time round.

Furthermore, it leads to a cumulative increase in the Eman (faith), goodness, knowledge and attentiveness of the heart and the feeling of ease in the breast, not to mention aiding the 'abd in getting rid of the traces of dirt from the heart just like a garment is washed over and over until it becomes clean. It is fascinating wisdom that astounds the mind and points to His Perfection, Mercy and Compassion. And it may be asserted that all we have mentioned above (of the virtues of Salah) is just a little bit in comparison to the vast knowledge we are unaware of, which is greater and superior.

Servitude in al-Tashahhud and the meaning of al-Tahiyyat

As the slave is about to conclude his Salah, it is prescribed for him to sit down before his Lord, to glorify Him and praise Him with all that befits Him;

Hence it is dictated for him to proclaim greetings (al-Tahiyyat) which befit Allah alone. It is the custom of kings to have people greeting them with different types of greetings, be it in words or actions, as a token of their deference and humility to them.

You would find some people praise them by words, some would prostrate to them, some would complement them, some would supplicate for their kingship to abide forever, and some people would do all the aforementioned; they prostrate to the king, then extol his praises, and then supplicate that his kingship last forever. However, as Allah is the true King whose Face is the only everlasting while everything else shall come to an end, it befits Him alone to receive the Supreme and Perfect Greetings embodied by al-Tahiyyat.

And it is for this reason that some scholars interpreted al-Tahiyyat to refer to His reign while other scholars interpreted it to affirm His everlasting kingship. The reality is as I have mentioned, it is an all-encompassing greeting that embraces all these aspects: His Reign, Ownership and Sovereignty. All these Attributes are ascribed to Allah (in the most perfect sense) and it befits Him even more because every greeting given to any king, be it a prostration or praise or a supplication for their lasting kinship, in fact, belongs to Allah.

That is why the word al-tahiyyat is prefixed by the definite article (*al*) that semantically indicates that these greetings encompass all greetings. And, the word itself is derived from another word (hayah) that means life; thus it affirms the perpetuity of the greeted.

This is similar to how they used to say to their kings: "We hope you live the life yet to come," or "We hope you have an everlasting life," or "We hope you live ten thousand years," and so forth. These are the roots of their statements (that we hear to this day): "I ask Allah to never cease your days and I ask Allah to lengthen your life," and so on and so forth... all these are used to mean continuation and prolongation of one's life or kingship. For this reason, all such expressions should be used for Allah alone because He is the All-Living, Self-Subsisting and Everlasting One. Next in these supreme greetings comes the word *al-sawlawat*, which affirms the exclusivity of Salah to Allah alone. It is for this reason, the word is used in a plural format and structured with the definite article (*al*) assert that anything that can be called Salah, be it exclusive or general, is for Allah alone and befits none except Him.

The wisdom behind interlinking al-Tahiyyat and al-Salawat

The wisdom behind interlinking these two words al-Tahiyyat and al-Salawat is that al-Tahiyyat belong to Allah alone as He has ownership of us and al-Salawat belong to Him as we are His slaves, and both of these are entitlements exclusive to Him; greetings are given to Him alone and prayers are intended for Him alone. Then the adjective word al-Tahiyyat (the good and pure) is used to qualify His Attributes and His Kingship. It conveys the meaning that He is Good, and so is His Speech, Actions and everything that comes from Him and attributed to Him or associated with His Names. That is to say, His Essence, His actions, His words, and all that He attributed or associated to Himself such as: His House, His Servant, His Spirit, are all good.

The meanings of all goodly statements al-Kalima al-Tayyib are His too as they encompass extolling, praising, glorifying and exalting Him with His Attributes and for His Graces such as saying: "You are glorified O Allah and praised! Your Name is Blessed; Your Majesty is Exalted and none has the right to be worshipped save You. Glorified is Allah and Praise and thanks be to Allah, and there is none worthy of worship save You and Allah is the Greatest. There is none worthy of worship save You, Allah is the Greatest, Glorified is Allah and Praise and thanks be to Allah."

All good emanates from Him and to Him it belongs; He is Good and accepts nothing but good. He is the Lord and the Ilāh of the good; and those who will neighbor Him in the house of honor (i.e. Paradise) are the good ones.

The Noblest words after the Quran

You ought to contemplate the best words and expressions that are second only to the Qur'an, such as: "Glory be to Allah, and to Him is all Praise, Glory be to Allah, the Most Perfect [and all Greatness is for Him]. There is no power or might except in Allah."

It is only then that you will realize that such words cannot be used to address anyone besides Allah. This is because "Subban Allah" denotes that Allah is far above any defect or shortcoming, and that His Attributes are far beyond those of His creation. As for "Alhamdulillāh," it testifies to the ultimate Perfection of His Words, Actions and Attributes. The words "La ilāh illAllah" affirm that He is the only Lord and llāh worthy of worship and everything else that is worshipped besides Allah is falsehood. He is the only true llāh.

Anyone who takes an Ilāh other than Him will be like a man who takes the (weak and fragile) house of spiders as his house, to which he retreats in hope of protecting himself from heat and cold, which surely shall not benefit him in the least. The words "Allahu Akbar" affirm that He is Greater, more supreme, prouder, more powerful and more knowledgeable than anyone or anything other than Him. This is why neither these words nor their underlying meanings are appropriate to use in reference to anyone or anything other Allah.

Servitude in al-Taslim

After greeting Allah, it is then prescribed for the 'abd to send greetings upon all the righteous slaves of Allah - the persons whom Allah has favoured and chosen.

This part of the greeting is positioned right after the greetings and praise of Allah, in conformation to the order mentioned in the ayah: *"Say, [O Muḥammad], Praise be to Allah, and peace upon His servants whom He has chosen. Is Allah better or what they associate with Him?"* *[27:59]*

$$\text{قُلِ ٱلْحَمْدُ لِلَّهِ وَسَلَٰمٌ عَلَىٰ عِبَادِهِ ٱلَّذِينَ ٱصْطَفَىٰٓ ءَآللَّهُ خَيْرٌ أَمَّا يُشْرِكُونَ ۝}$$

Not to mention that since it is a greeting intended for the created, (therefore as a matter of etiquette) it should not precede the greetings addressed to the Creator. Within the greeting intended for His righteous slaves, Allah has prescribed that they be addressed in order of the ranks of the recipients, so that the first to be greeted is the one who deserves it the most: the Prophet, Muḥammad, peace and blessings be upon him, whose nation received every form of good only through him. The second person to be greeted is the slave himself followed by the rest of the pious slaves of Allah, the best among whom are the Prophets and the Angels followed by the Companions of the Prophet and then the followers of all Prophets, and all the righteous slaves occupying the heavens and the earth. At the end, it is prescribed for him to send salutations of peace upon all those who deserve to be greeted, in particular and in general.

The Meaning of the two Shahadahs in al-Tahiyyat

Then it is prescribed for the 'abd to bear witness and declare the testimony of truth upon which the Salah is built, a well a one of its rights upon him; that is to say, if he does not testify, the Salah will be of no benefit to him.

This is to testify that Allah revealed to His Messenger the Message (i.e. Islam). With this testimony, the Salah is finished, as per the statement of Abdullah ibn Mas'ud (RA): "After you say it (i.e. the two testimonies), your Salah will have been finished; you have the choice then to either get up or remain sitting down." But this word (i.e. finish) can be interpreted linguistically to mean that the Salah finishes after the testimony has been said, as under-stood by the people of Kufa, or to mean that the Salah is about to finish, as understood by the people of Hijaz. In both cases, the testimony of truth is positioned at the end of the Salah similar to how it is prescribed to be the seal of wudu and of life (i.e. it is prescribed to be pronounced at the end of wudu and at the end of one's life too).

The Prophet, peace and blessings be upon him, said: "Whosever's last words before he dies were that there is no llāh worthy of worship except Allah, will enter Paradise." After having concluded the Salah, the 'abd is permitted to ask Allah for anything he wants.

Sending al-Salat upon the Prophet, Peace and Blessings Be Upon Him

It is prescribed for him to intercede by sending Salah upon the Prophet, peace and blessings be upon him, before he starts beseeching Allah for his needs, because sending Salah upon the Prophet, peace and blessings be upon him, is one of the most important intercessory means to be utilized before invoking Allah. It is reported in the Sunan books of hadith that Fudalah ibn 'Ubayd (RA) narrated that the Messenger of Allah, peace and blessings be upon him, said:

"If any one of you prays, he should commence by glorifying his Lord and praising Him; he should invoke peace and blessings on the Prophet, peace and blessings be upon him, and thereafter he should supplicate to Allah for anything he wishes."

This supplication comes at the end of the Salah after the greetings and the Salah upon the Messenger of Allah, peace and blessings be upon him; thereafter the 'abd has the choice and freedom to ask Allah for what he wants.

The Sunnah of the Adhan

This is similar to what has been prescribed for the 'abd to do upon hearing the adhān;

(1) To repeat the phrases uttered during the adhān

(2) To say at its conclusion: I am content and pleased that Allah is my Lord, Islam is my religion, and Mūhammad is the Messenger

(3) To ask Allah to grant the Prophet the right of intercession and ascendancy and to grant him on the Day of Judgment the best and the highest place in Paradise that was promised

(4) Then to send Salah upon him

(5) And finally to ask Allah for his needs

The prescribed five acts mentioned above should never be over-looked.

The Messenger of Allah, peace and blessings be upon him, heard a man supplicating in prayer. He did not glorify Allah and neither did he invoke blessings on the Prophet, peace and blessings be upon him. The Messenger of Allah, peace and blessings be upon him, said: "He made haste."

He then called him and said to him or to those around him: "If any one of you prays, he should commence by glorifying his Lord and praising Him; he should invoke peace and blessings on the Prophet, peace and blessings be upon him, and thereafter he should supplicate to Allah for anything he wishes."

"Beware of preoccupying your heart with what it has not been created for."

-- Ibn Qayyim Al-Jawziyya

"If you knew the true value of yourself, you will never allow yourself to be humiliated by committing sins."

"Eman is of two halves; half is patience (Sabr) and half is being thankful (Shukr)."

"He who keeps his heart near God will find peace and tranquility, whilst he who gives his heart to the people will find restlessness and apprehension."

"How strange! You lose a little from you and you cry. And your whole life is wasting and you're laughing"

"Be to Allah as He wishes, and He will be to you more than you can wish for."

"Patience is that the heart does not feel anger towards that which is destined and that the mouth does not complain."

"One of the most beneficial of remedies is persisting in duâ."

Chapter Two

The Secret of Salah lies in devotion to Allah

The secret and the essence of Salah is to devote oneself to Allah while praying -just as the slave should not turn his face away from the direction of the Qiblah, he should also disallow his heart from giving attention to anything except his Lord. Therefore the 'abd should let the Ka'bah - the House of Allah - be the direction of his body and face, and let Allah be the direction of his heart and soul. Allah shall give His attention to His 'abd in proportion to the level of his devotion and focus in Salah. Therefore, if he turns away from Allah (by becoming unmindful), Allah too shall turn away from him - truly, as you judge, shall you yourself be judged. *"We have certainly seen the turning of your face toward the heaven, and We will surely turn you to a qiblah with which you will be pleased.*

So turn your face toward al-Masjid al-Haram. And wherever you [believers] are, turn your faces toward it [in prayer]. Indeed, those who have been given the Scripture well know that it is the truth from their Lord. And Allah is not unaware of what they do."

قَدْ نَرَىٰ تَقَلُّبَ وَجْهِكَ فِى ٱلسَّمَآءِ فَلَنُوَلِّيَنَّكَ قِبْلَةً تَرْضَىٰهَا فَوَلِّ وَجْهَكَ شَطْرَ ٱلْمَسْجِدِ ٱلْحَرَامِ وَحَيْثُ مَا كُنتُمْ فَوَلُّواْ وُجُوهَكُمْ شَطْرَهُۥ وَإِنَّ ٱلَّذِينَ أُوتُواْ ٱلْكِتَٰبَ لَيَعْلَمُونَ أَنَّهُ ٱلْحَقُّ مِن رَّبِّهِمْ وَمَا ٱللَّهُ بِغَٰفِلٍ عَمَّا يَعْمَلُونَ ﴿١٤٤﴾

Devotion to Allah in Salah is of three levels

(1) Devotion of the heart: This level safeguards the heart and rectifies its affairs from the sickness of desires and the whispers of Satan, as well as all thoughts that may nullify his Salah or lessen its reward.

(2) Devotion of ihsan: This level is when the 'abd is mindful of Allah in his Salah to the degree that he becomes as if he worships Him while seeing Him.

(3) Devotion of understanding: This level is reached when the slave reflects upon and comprehends the meanings of the words of Allah (i.e. Quran) that he recites. And, when he contemplates the details of the worship (i.e. Salah) in order to pay its due right in humility and tranquility.

If the slave successfully reaches these three levels, he will have truly established and performed his Salah in the most perfect manner and in return, he will receive the full attention of Allah.

Devotion in Salah

The devotion of standing upright before Allah in Salah comes into effect when the slave devotes his attention to the Greatness of Allah and His Attribute of Self-subsistence, as this will ensure that he turns neither his face nor his eyes from side to side. The devotion of the statement: *"Allah is the Greatest"* by which the slave commences the Salah is realized when the slave devotes his attention and focus to His Pride, Glory and Exaltation. The devotion of the opening supplication happens when the servant extols and glorifies and praises Him profusely, ascribing to Him all that befits Him and declares His transcendence above everything that does not befit Him, and praises Him for His Attributes and Perfection.

The devotion of taking refuge in Allah from the accursed Satan is realized by having confidence and faith that Allah shall support him, protect him and aid him against Satan.

The devotion of reciting the Quran lies in the slave's endeavor to learn about Allah through His Words as if trying to see Him through His revelation. One of the righteous Salaf said: "Allah manifests Himself to His slaves through His Speech (i.e. Quran)." It is, however, the case that the degree of devotion while reciting and praying varies from one person to another, and the difference between them is like the difference between the one whose both eyes are sound and unimpaired, and the one-eyed individual, the blind person, the deaf person, etc. in their levels of perception.

The 'abd should be as heedful as possible to His Essence, Attributes, Actions, Commandments, Laws and Names.

The devotion of bowing down is contained in being mindful to the Greatness and the Pride of Allah, Exalted be He. For that reason it is prescribed for him to say while he is in the state of bowing down: Glory to my Lord, the Most High."

After he rises up from his bowing stance, he should focus his attention upon glorifying and praising Allah repeatedly, so as to manifest his servitude to Him, the One in whose Hand is the sole authority to bestow and deny.

When the servant falls into prostration, he ought to focus his attention on feeling his nearness to Him, overwhelmed in humility in the hope that He forgives him, guides him, sustains him, protects him and bestows His mercy upon him. Then, when he raises his head and adopts the sitting posture, his inner condition takes on a different nature, one that is similar to the condition of the pilgrim when he performs the last circumambulation because at that point, his heart begins to realize that he is about to complete his prayer and with it leave this blessed condition that he is experiencing, and that soon he will be returning to the dreariness of his worldly affairs that he had detached himself from just before standing before his Lord. Once again he will be subject to the feelings of pain and anguish that his heart endured before he started praying, all of which melted away as soon as he commenced his Salah.

At that point, his heart rushes to enjoy the nearness of Allah for the last time, to bask in His grace, and to be saved from the disruptiveness of his worldly affairs. The feeling of bitterness he endures is due to his recognition that all this lasts only as long as he is praying. At this stage, the heart cannot but feel burdened and troubled knowing that all this is about to end and that he is about to return to these worldly affairs and concerns. This agitates the 'abd to the point that he starts wishing that this Salah were the final act of his life. Not to mention the slave's awareness that as soon as he finishes praying he will resume communicating with those who bring him nothing but concerns, worries and harm after he had been invoking and supplicating his Lord. However, this kind of feeling cannot be experienced except by those whose hearts are alive with the remembrance and love of Allah and who are cognizant of the negative effect that mankind leaves on their hearts. This is because interacting with people puts him in the way of harm and worries, agitates his heart and makes him overlook or miss good deeds, not to mention causing him to commit more sins. More importantly, it distracts him from invoking Allah, the most High.

Discussion on Taslim

The 'abd (of Allah) is either exposed to:

(1) The universally decreed Judgment of Allah pertaining to his inward and outward conditions, which necessitates him to act in accordance with his state of servitude and slavery to Allah, since each judgment is associated with a special condition of servitude to Allah.

(2) The actions that the 'abd performs out of his servitude to Allah and these necessitate the judgments that ensue from the prescribed religious commandments.

Each of these aspects necessitate that the 'abd (of Allah) submits himself to Allah, Exalted be He. In fact, this is the reason for naming him a Muslim, with reference to Islam - which is derived from the word taslim, which means submission. As the slave submits to the divine law of his Lord as well as His universally decreed Judgment by demonstrating his servitude to Him and abstaining from following his own desires and sins, he will be as if he's saying: I am destined to bear the title of Islam deservedly.

Exposition on the fruits al-Khushu

After his heart has been filled with tranquility through the remembrance of Allah, recitation of His Words, expressing his love for Him as well as demonstrating his servitude to Him, he leans towards his Lord and draws closer to Him to find peace, receiving safety and peace through his Eman and experiencing hap-piness through his Ihsan. It is for this reason that, abiding by these two ideals is of utmost necessity, failing this he shall neither enjoy life, success nor happiness. However, because the slave has been tried with an innate nature that entices him to commit sins, base desires that serve the callings of his innate nature, not to mention the seductive whispers of Satan, all of which aim to waste his share of his reward or, at the very least, decrease his share of the reward, the wisdom of Allah, the Most Merciful and the Mighty, has decreed for him the Salah, to compensate him for the missed reward and to revive his willpower and rectify his Eman. The Mercy and Wisdom of Allah manifest themselves again when He, Exalted be He, Decreed a period of time to pass between five prayers so that the slave can regain his composure and blot out the sins he earned in between.

Furthermore, He made the actions of Salah such that they symbolize his submission, surrender and humility to Allah; thus He made for each body limb a duty to perform what demonstrates its servitude to Allah. He also made the spirit of Salah and the means to reap its fruits that the slave give his full attention and complete devotion to Allah. And he made its reward and place be when he enters upon Allah (i.e. commences Salah) and

He ordered his 'abd to adorn himself before commencing the Salah as a reminder for him of the Day of Judgment when he shall be screened for questioning.

The fruit of Salah is true devotion to Allah

The fruit of fasting is the purification of the soul. The fruit of Zakah (obligatory alms) is the purification of wealth. The fruit of Hajj (pilgrimage) is forgiveness. The fruit of jihad (fighting is submitting the soul) that Allah bartered from His servants in exchange for Paradise. The fruit of Salah is the attention of the 'abd upon his Lord and the attention of Allah given to His 'abd.

However embarking towards Allah with complete devotion in Salah encompasses all the aforementioned fruits because the fruits of all good deeds are found when the 'abd embarks towards Allah with true devotion.

This explains why the Prophet, peace and blessings be upon him, never said, my comfort lies in fasting, or Hajj, or al-umrah or any other good deed but rather he said: "my comfort has been made in the Salah." It is also worthwhile to pay attention to the Prophet's choice of words in this statement. He said "my comfort is made in Salah" and did not say "my comfort is made with Salah" because the former means that comfort is achieved only after commencing the Salah, while the latter implies that such comfort is received even when not praying.

This is why when he sought the comfort of his heart he would say: "O Bilal, call for Salah: give us comfort by it."

Why Salah gives us comfort?

Meaning, call for the prayer so that we can pray and relieve our- selves from the hardships of this life, just as how a tired person finds repose as soon as he arrives at his house and settles down in it, breaking away from the hardships and the fatigue he endured outside. You ought to pause and reflect again upon his choice of words that reveal another subtlety; the Prophet, peace and blessings be upon him, did not say, let us relieve ourselves from the burden of duty (i.e. Salah), which is the attitude of those who pray just to release themselves from the obligation of praying, who feel hassled every time they have to pray - and when they pray they cannot wait to finish it.

This because the source of their comfort is found outside the Salah, since their hearts are filled with everything except Allah. Thus, praying merely keeps them from indulging in this worldly life that they love so much. They are easily observed from their manner of performing prayer; they pray in a rush and lack tranquility and calmness. The only thing that compels them to pray in the first place is that they know it is a must (obligation). However, their Salah is deficient; they utter with their tongues that which does not conform to what is in their hearts. All the while, the voice of their heart echoes their desire, let's get this Salah over with! Therefore the difference between a person whose comfort is found in the Salah and a person whose comfort is found outside the Salah is obvious and self-evident.

The former finds Salah to be a grace upon his heart through which he experiences tranquility, calmness and pleasure, whereas the latter finds Salah akin to heavy chains shackling his limbs and a gloomy cell imprisoning his heart. Truly, those whose comfort is not found in Salah feel as if praying was a prison for their soul and chains confining their limbs from committing sins. Despite that, the Salah of this type of people might be a means whereby their sins are forgiven and they receive a share of Allah's Mercy depending on how much servitude to Allah they manage to demonstrate while praying. But on the other hand, it is also possible they might be punished for the deficiency in their Salah. As for those whose comfort is to be found in Salah, for them praying is the garden in which they find comfort, pleasure, tranquility, and the grace of their hearts and souls.

It brings them nearer to Allah and elevates their rank, so that they only have a reward similar to those that preceded, but they also enjoy a special rank that none ever had, by being brought near to Allah, in addition to the mere reward they receive for the performance of their Salah.

From the benefits of Salah is nearness to Allah

It is customary for kings to promise reward and nearness to those whom they are pleased with. *"And when the magicians arrived, they said to Pharaoh, "Is there indeed for us a reward if we are the predominant?"* [26:41]

فَلَمَّا جَاءَ ٱلسَّحَرَةُ قَالُوا لِفِرْعَوْنَ أَئِنَّ لَنَا لَأَجْرًا إِن كُنَّا نَحْنُ ٱلْغَٰلِبِينَ ﴿٤١﴾

And he answered that they would be rewarded and be among those near to him, saying: *"He said, "Yes, and, [moreover], you will be among those made near [to me]."* *[7:114]*

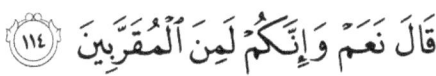

The example of the first type is like a man who entered the abode of the king but was unable to gain entrance to him as there was a barrier standing between him and the Icing, hence he was unable to see him or gain access to this person. The barrier is an embodiment of his desires and lusts as well as the smoke screen of his hopeful wishes in this life; his heart is sick and his self is wrapped up in what it desires wanting only its immediate share in this life. It is for these reasons that all the while they pray they are in an unhappy state wherein they are not only unable to obtain any comfort, but are also empty of feelings of fear and hope in Allah, which makes prayer a suffering for them that only ceases when they finish praying, as only then are they able to return to that in which they find their comfort (i.e. worldly affairs and pleasures).

The example of the second type is like a man who entered the house of the king upon which the barrier screening him from the king is removed; thus he is able to find delight in looking at the king and being at his service and in his obedience. In return, the king lavishes upon him every form of grace and brings him near to him himself. For all these reasons, he is unable to bear leaving the house and wishes to remain standing before him to enjoy the sweetness of being close to him, the tranquility that he experiences from it, and being held in esteem by Allah while he basks in His good Words (i.e. Quran).

He also enjoys being in such a state of humbleness and humility before Him, for which he invokes Him more and more while he is being showered with His graces from every direction, not to mention the calmness that his soul experiences while his heart and limbs are fully attentive to his Lord. He is pleased and comfortable, worshipping Allah as if he sees Him, for He manifest Himself to him through His Words (i.e. Quran). It should thus come as no surprise that the most distressing thing for him is to have to leave all that (i.e. conclude the Salah). And Allah is the Guide and the Helper.

The aforementioned are just some brief glimpses and hints about Salah and a disclosure of some of its subtle qualities and hidden gems.

"Every gulp of air that goes out in a cause other than the cause of Allah will turn to sorrow and regret on the Day of Judgement."

"And to have spent the night sleeping and awoken regretful, is better than to have spent the night standing (in prayer) and awaken impressed with oneself!"

"Ibn Taymiyyah lived poorly. He was imprisoned and threatened. But I have never seen anyone as happy as him."

"And verily for everything that a slave loses there is a substitute, but the one who loses Allah will never find anything to replace Him."

"Be sincere in your aim and you will find the support of Allaah surrounding you."

Chapter Three

Distinction between the people of al-Samā and the people of Salah

I call upon the people (al-Samā) who indulge themselves in listening (to music and songs) and I ask them by Allah, the One and only truthful llāh worthy of worship, to tell me if the experience and enjoyment they attain from listening to songs could ever be equal to, or even vaguely similar to, such feelings and state of heart! I ask them, by Allah, to tell me whether their indulgence in songs allows them at all to experience these sublime emotions and state of heart when they pray? In fact, I would like to know if they have ever even detected from afar the fragrance of such sublime emotions and experiences! I will take the liberty of answering these questions on their behalf.

The experience and enjoyment attained from praying is incongruous with, and bears not an iota of resemblance to the experience and enjoyment they attain from listening to songs. I fear that I might end up writing a long chapter, otherwise I would have mentioned some of what they experience when listening to songs, in order to explain the nature of this type of listening. A person whose heart has life in it and who enjoys even a minimal level of understanding shall realize the difference between the experience and enjoyment attained from reciting the Words of Allah (i.e. Quran) and the enjoyment attained from singing lyrics. You can recognize the difference between the experience and enjoyment attained from standing before Allah, the Lord of all the worlds (in Salah) and the enjoyment attained from standing before singers (and musicians).

You will also understand the difference between the experience and enjoyment attained from comprehending the meanings of the Words of Allah and the experience and enjoyment they attain from singing and enrapturement, which is the spell of fornication and the Quran of Satan. By Allah, whenever the love of both tastes (i.e. Quran and songs) enters the heart of a person, only one of them can remain in the heart as one of them will expel the other; just as the daughter of the Messenger of Allah, peace and blessings be upon him, and the daughter of the enemy of Allah cannot ever be married at the same time to one man. And Allah, Exalted be He, Knows best.

"The heart becomes sick, as the body becomes sick, and its remedy is al-Tawbah (repentance) and protection [from transgression]. It becomes rusty as a mirror becomes rusty, and its clarity is

obtained by remembrance. It becomes naked as the body becomes naked, and its beautification is al-Taqwa. It becomes hungry and thirsty as the body becomes hungry, and its food and drink are knowledge, love, dependence, repentance and servitude."

"A real man is one who fears the death of his heart, not of his body. Every drop of sweat and every breath we take in life, if not taken for the sake of Allah, will lead to regret and sorrow on the Day of Judgment"

"There is no joy for someone who has no sorrow. There is no pleasure for the one who has no patience No bliss for someone with no misery and no rest for the one with no fatigue. When someone is a little tired, he has long rest. When he endures the difficulty of steadfastness for a time that leads him to eternal life. All that the people of eternal bliss are in is steadfastness for a time."

Chapter Four

The Quran is the Best Music

It is only when the hearts that have deviated far from the guidance of the Prophet, peace and blessings be upon him, and have abandoned what he, his Companions and the righteous Salaf were upon, become upright that they will regain the discernment through which they can experience the right enjoyment and sensation. The early generations used to find enjoyment in matters pertaining to Allah, Exalted be He, such as: praying, reciting the Quran, contemplating on the Words of Allah and listening to them, attending the assemblies of scholars and the gatherings of knowledge, fighting in battles for the sake of Allah, enjoining the good and forbidding the wrong- doing, loving and despising people for the sake of Allah, etc.

However, the preference of the later generations, except those whom Allah saved, became distorted and they sought enjoyment in musical instruments, songs, dancing, noise and clamour, while desisting from doing deeds that Allah loves. Indeed, the experience and enjoyment attained from melodies is nothing like the experience and enjoyment attained from the Quran. The experience and enjoyment attained from musical instruments is nothing like the experience and enjoyment attained from reciting al-Nur and al-Mu'minun. The experience and enjoyment attained from tunes is nothing like the experience and enjoyment attained from the al-Zumar, and the experience and enjoyment obtained from flutes is nothing like the experience and enjoyment attained from the ayah: *"The Hour has come near, and the moon has split [in two]." [54:1]*

$$\text{اقْتَرَبَتِ ٱلسَّاعَةُ وَٱنشَقَّ ٱلْقَمَرُ ﴿١﴾}$$

The experience and enjoyment attained from woodwinds is definitely nothing like the experience and enjoyment attained from the Yasin and al-Saffat. The experience and enjoyment attained from saying poetry is nothing like the experience and enjoyment attained from reciting al-Shu'ara. The experience and enjoyment of whistlers and hand-clappers is nothing like the experience and enjoyment of al-Anbiya'. The experience and enjoyment attained from listening to songs and poetry describing the beauty of the eyes of women, their hips and bodies is nothing like the experience and enjoyment gained from listening to the Yunus and Hud. The experience and enjoyment of those who stand on their feet serving Satan is in nothing at all like the experience and enjoyment of those who stand on their feet serving the most

Merciful while reciting al-An'am and al-Ar'af. The experience and enjoyment of those in rapture upon being overwhelmed by music is nothing like the experience and enjoyment of the knower ('arif) when listening to the Great Quran and, in particular, when listening to al-Fatihah. And, the experience and enjoyment of those who jostle in Satan's barn to listen to music is nothing like the experience and enjoyment of those who crowd before the Most Merciful. Exalted is Allah for differentiating those bestowed with divine sublime emotions from those with earthly elation, in order to distinguish between those who are expelled [from Allah's Mercy] and the [true] servants [of Allah]. Indeed, He is above all defects and shortcomings; He sustains both types of individuals in this world, but only upon His [true] slaves shall He bestow honour and grace on the Day of Judgment.

By Allah, the love to hear the Quran of Satan and the love to hear the Words of the most Merciful shall never coexist in one heart, just as how the daughter of the enemy of Allah and the daughter of the Messenger of Allah, peace and blessings be upon him, cannot be with the same man ever. As the poet said: *"You shall die for the one whom you love... Therefore, find yourself the lover who is most favourable to you."*

Al-Sama' of the people of Truth

When the Companions of the Messenger of Allah, peace and blessings be upon him, got together and wanted their hearts to be moved and to feel some ease and comfort to lighten their burden, they would ask one of them to recite the Qur'an while the rest listened to him with rapt attention. And so, their selves would be overwhelmed with tranquility and their eyes would overflow with tears, and their hearts would taste the sweetness of Eman (faith), which is far beyond what those who listen to songs could ever experience.

'Umar ibn al-Khattab (RA) used to say to Abu Musa al-Ash'ari (RA) whenever he was in his company: "O Abu Musa, remind us of our Lord" and as soon as he would start reciting Quran, their hearts would be touched and deeply moved. 'Uthman ibn 'Affan (RA) used to say: "If our hearts were pure, we would never have enough of the Words of Allah."

It is true, indeed. How can a person ever be satisfied when it comes to the words of the one whom he loves and with whom his hopes and aspirations lie! How can a man be sufficient when it comes to Quran with which the Salah is commenced, not with crass melodies and singing!

As the poet said: *"When we fall ill we seek cure in your remembrance... such that whenever we cease it, we become more sick."*

The people of melodies and songs are segregated from the people of the Quran, as each group lives in a different domain of sphere. Truly, the condition of the one who is enraptured by listening to songs is nothing compared to the condition of sublime elation and enjoyment that is experienced by the one listening to the Qur'an while his heart enjoys the sweet taste of Eman. He experiences a state of tranquility, ease and amiability and a longing in his heart to meet His Lord, and a readiness to understand the meanings of His Words and to apply what he understands on himself. All this impels him to recite His Words beautifully and perfectly. You find him reciting:

Ta, Ha. We have not sent down to you the Qur'an that you be distressed. But only as a reminder for those who fear [Allah] - A revelation from He who created the earth and highest heavens. The Most Merciful [who is] above the Throne established. To Him belongs what is in the heavens and what is on the earth and what is between them and what is under the soil. And if you speak aloud - then indeed, He knows the secret and what is [even] more hidden. [20:1-7]

طه ۞

مَآ أَنزَلْنَا عَلَيْكَ ٱلْقُرْءَانَ لِتَشْقَىٰٓ ۞

إِلَّا تَذْكِرَةً لِّمَن يَخْشَىٰ ۞

تَنزِيلًا مِّمَّنْ خَلَقَ ٱلْأَرْضَ وَٱلسَّمَٰوَٰتِ ٱلْعُلَى ۞

ٱلرَّحْمَٰنُ عَلَى ٱلْعَرْشِ ٱسْتَوَىٰ ۞

لَهُۥ مَا فِى ٱلسَّمَٰوَٰتِ وَمَا فِى ٱلْأَرْضِ وَمَا بَيْنَهُمَا وَمَا تَحْتَ ٱلثَّرَىٰ ۞

وَإِن تَجْهَرْ بِٱلْقَوْلِ فَإِنَّهُۥ يَعْلَمُ ٱلسِّرَّ وَأَخْفَى ۞

And other ayat of this theme, whose effect on the heart will be like the effect of communicating with the love of one's life after a long absence - as long as the heart is sincere and is truly alive, and has smelled the fragrance of loving Allah and has tasted its sweetness. The effect (of reciting or listening to the Quran) upon him is like a drink of cold water after having felt severe thirst in very hot weather, or like land just after life-giving rains have fallen upon it after it had been parched and arid, causing the land to grow every nice variety of plant that stand tall in the land thanking and praising Him. After all this, it should be clear that in the Sight of Allah, His Angels, His Prophets and His truthful and sincere servants, the rank of those listening to the Quran and the feeling they experience from it shall never equal the rank. They shall be far above the rank of those listening to music and what they experience out of it.

This is because the people of music and songs are the servants of their own lustful souls and desires; they listen only to entertain their lustful souls and earn their share of falsehood. Whosoever is unable to distinguish the difference between the Quran and listening to music and songs, and is unable to distinguish between the transcendent experience attained from the Quran and the base experience attained from music, should ask his Lord, sincerely and truthfully, to revive his heart and to grant him a light to illuminate the depths of his ignorance, and to bestow him with the ability to differentiate between the truth and the falsehood. Indeed, He is near and answers the prayers of His servants.

"As you can taste a pot full of food with a spoon likewise someone's tongue can tell you about his heart." -- Ibn Qayyim Al-Jawziyya

Chapter Five

The Types of Hearts

There is a subtle sensation that only the people habituated to music and songs can perceive and experience after listening to songs and then departing from that environment. The state of elation and rapture they experience while listening to music and songs is always followed by a state of their heart feeling troubled (tired), accompanied by feelings of desolation and darkness. However, it is only those whose hearts still retain a minimal level of life who will be able to notice this subtle change, as opposed to those whose hearts are completely dead, because the dead cannot feel the pain of wounds. If they were ever asked about what provoked these uncomfortable feelings, they would not be able to tell because their hearts are steeped in their corrupt appetites.

Not only are they unable to realize the root cause behind the pain they endure, they are also unable to comprehend how they ever came to have such corrupted heart - although if they weighed what they experience from music and songs in the scales of knowledge, they would be able to grasp the causes and reasons. But I shall communicate the causes of such feelings of abnormality, constriction and desolation to you.

And of the people is he who buys the amusement of speech to mislead [others] from the way of Allah without knowledge and who takes it in ridicule. Those will have a humiliating punishment. [31:16]

وَمِنَ ٱلنَّاسِ مَن يَشْتَرِى لَهْوَ ٱلْحَدِيثِ لِيُضِلَّ عَن سَبِيلِ ٱللَّهِ بِغَيْرِ عِلْمٍ وَيَتَّخِذَهَا هُزُوًا أُوْلَٰٓئِكَ لَهُمْ عَذَابٌ مُّهِينٌ ۝

Consider under the best circumstances, listening to poems and songs consists of partaking in a mixture of truth and falsehood - a combination of desires and dubiety. And even in the best case, the condition of the one who engages in listening to songs and poems is that his soul takes it share of what might be deemed commended in religion, except that it has been adulterated by his whims and the whispers of Satan, effectively making what he acquires from his listening to be neither pure nor clean. In other words, the positive and beneficial aspect of listening to songs, that the Most Merciful deems acceptable, will be tainted with the negative and condemned aspect of it that is to Satan's liking. Ultimately, the heart ends up receiving a share of good and a share of evil. And this is the best possible scenario with listening to songs, as it is founded on lustful wishes, desires and Satanic inclinations.

Although it has a bit of goodness in it. It will be like a small amount of pure water dribbling down the valley of the heart that has encountered a torrent of impure water causing the impure to prevail, or at the very least having the divine inspiration to run alongside the satanic inspiration.

Despite the inability of the heart in which a modicum of sincerity still prevails in recognizing the feeling of disquiet caused by listening to music, particularly when the soul is submerged in music and songs and has been taken off-course from pursuing its objective -as soon as the heart awakes from this state of intoxication after having put a distance between itself and the enjoyment obtained from music and songs it endures feelings of distress, isolation and annoyance.

The more sincere and truthful the heart is, the more it is able to recognize this effect because the sentience of the heart dictates feeling the negative impact of listening to music and songs even without realizing the cause behind these negative feelings. This situation has many parallels in real life; consider the example of a person, whose attention is focused on his lust, or who sees something he fears, or is busy indulging in an activity that he enjoys, which overtakes his heart and senses -he will not feel any slap, bites or stings that he (might) receive while in this condition. Yet as soon as he emerges out from this state of focus or pleasure, he starts feeling the pain of the hit or sting as if he had just received it. This is due to him being in a state that prevented him from sensing pain, but when the reason preventing him from feeling pain was removed, he starts to experience the pain.

This is the reason that compelled some of the truthful ones to rush to renew their repentance and seek Allah's forgiveness as soon as they stopped listening to songs and music, and to look for the means to cure their state of aloofness (from Allah) and strange- ness (that had resulted from their listening to songs and music). This state is perceived and recognized by those with sound reasoning and intellect and whose objective is to perfect their souls and learn the ills and remedies of their hearts - And Allah is Whom we ask for help.

While it is undeniable that listening to poetry with the right intention might leave a positive and commendable effect on the heart, it would be akin to a person who drinks honey using a dirty cup.

The truthful and sincere ones with lofty aspirations find them- selves above drinking from a cup they find dirty, as their uprightness, purity and high endeavor makes them balk at the idea, and they only agree to drink in a clean cup, even if it means they have to wait for a long time. On the other hand, some people will drink in any cup they find, even if this cup is made of the bones of dead animals or pigskin or dog skin, or even if the cup is normally used to consume alcohol from, making the excuse that he is not drinking alcohol in it. Indeed, even crows recoil from drinking from such utensils, even if they are offered the best drink in them. If the truthful one could isolate this (negative feeling) during his attendance of poetry and singing, he would have realized it, but the sweetness of honey causes him to overlook the dirt and filth of the cup.

However, as soon as he concludes his listening, he endures a state of strangeness and constriction in his heart - but this only happens if he is truthful with Allah and if he listened to songs and poetry (assuming it to be) for the sake of Allah. As for the liar whose intention in listening is for enjoyment and to fulfill his base desires, he is like a person drinking impure drink from a dirty cup and yet unable to perceive the ill-feelings mentioned above, because Satan and his lustful desires have taken over his heart. On the other hand, the ones whose interest and heart lies in listening to the Quran, he will be drinking a pure, unadulterated drink in the purest and cleanest of cups.

The drinking cups are of three types: pure and clean, impure and dirty and a mixture of both.

And drinks are of three types as well: pure, impure and a mixture of the two.

The Types of Hearts

Hearts are of three kinds:

(1) Healthy hearts, whose drink is pure and whose drinking cups are clean,

(2) Sick hearts whose drinks are impure and whose drinking cups are filthy, and

(3) Hearts that contain elements of both Eman and hypocrisy that drink from both pure and impure cups. Allah measures everything; the perceptive one is he who looks deeply into causal factors and contemplates their outcomes and objectives.

The one who understands the underlying objectives of religious legislations -in particular the principle of blocking the means that lead to matters the religion prohibits - will certainly declare listening to songs and poetry to be impermissible, especially considering that listening to the singing of a non-mahram woman, looking at her as well as being in private with her are in themselves unlawful.

The matters that religion prohibits fall into two categories:

(1) Matters that are prohibited due to the corruption and evil that they involve (in themselves).

(2) Matters that are made prohibited because they serve as a means to what is deemed evil or corrupted.

That is why a person who only looks into the apparent aspect of whether listening to poetry and singing is allowed or not, with- out considering what it can lead up to, might find this ruling debatable or hard to fathom. And Allah, most High, Knows best.

To conclude, all praise be to Allah, the Lord of all worlds, alone, and may the Salah and Salam of Allah be upon the master of all the Prophets, Mūhammad, peace and blessings be upon him, and upon his Family, his Companions, and their followers until the Day of Judgment. Indeed, everything is with Your Favour and Help exclusively, for You are the Most Merciful.

"O you who sold yourself for the sake of something that will cause you suffering and pain, and which will also lose its beauty, you sold the most precious item for the cheapest price, as if you neither knew the value of the goods nor the meanness of the prize. Wait until you come on the Day of Mutual Loss and Gain and you will discover the injustice of this contract."

"From the perfection of Allah's ihsan is that He allows His slave to taste the bitterness of the break before the sweetness of the mend. So He does not break his believing slave, except to mend him. And He does not withhold from him, except to give him. And He does not test him (with hardship), except to cure him."

"O you, who spends his lifetime disobeying his Lord, no one amongst your enemies is wicked to you more than you are to yourself"

APPENDIX I

Ibn al-Qayyim on Khushu

Allah, Most High, says: *"Has the time not come for those who have believed that their hearts should become humbly submissive at the remembrance of Allah and what has come down of the truth? And let them not be like those who were given the Scripture before, and a long period passed over them, so their hearts hardened; and many of them are defiantly disobedient."* [57:16]

﴿أَلَمْ يَأْنِ لِلَّذِينَ ءَامَنُوٓاْ أَن تَخْشَعَ قُلُوبُهُمْ لِذِكْرِ ٱللَّهِ وَمَا نَزَلَ مِنَ ٱلْحَقِّ وَلَا يَكُونُواْ كَٱلَّذِينَ أُوتُواْ ٱلْكِتَٰبَ مِن قَبْلُ فَطَالَ عَلَيْهِمُ ٱلْأَمَدُ فَقَسَتْ قُلُوبُهُمْ وَكَثِيرٌ مِّنْهُمْ فَٰسِقُونَ ۝١٦﴾

Ibn Mas'ud (RA) said: "The time between our accepting Islam and being rebuked by this verse was four years."

Ibn 'Abbas said: "Allah granted time and leeway to the hearts of the believers, then, at the turn of the thirteenth year after the revelation had started, He rebuked them."

Allah, Most High, says: *"Certainly will the believers have succeeded: They who are during their prayer humbly submissive. [23:1-2]*

$$قَدْ أَفْلَحَ ٱلْمُؤْمِنُونَ ۝١$$

$$ٱلَّذِينَ هُمْ فِي صَلَاتِهِمْ خَاشِعُونَ ۝٢$$

Linguistically, khushu' means sinking, subservience, and stillness. Allah, Most High, says: *"That Day, everyone will follow [the call of] the Caller [with] no deviation therefrom, and [all] voices will be stilled before the Most Merciful, so you will not hear except a whisper [of footsteps]." [20:108]*

يَوْمَئِذٍ يَتَّبِعُونَ ٱلدَّاعِىَ لَا عِوَجَ لَهُۥۖ وَخَشَعَتِ ٱلْأَصْوَاتُ لِلرَّحْمَٰنِ فَلَا تَسْمَعُ إِلَّا هَمْسًا ۝

i.e. stilled and humbled. In this respect, the earth has been described as having khushu', i.e. its being dry, bare, and low and not being elevated with plant and vegetation. Allah, Most High, says:

"And of His signs is that you see the earth stilled, but when We send down upon it rain, it quivers and grows. Indeed, He who has given it life is the Giver of Life to the dead. Indeed, He is over all things competent." [41:39]

وَمِنْ ءَايَٰتِهِۦٓ أَنَّكَ تَرَى ٱلْأَرْضَ خَٰشِعَةً فَإِذَآ أَنزَلْنَا عَلَيْهَا ٱلْمَآءَ ٱهْتَزَّتْ وَرَبَتْۚ إِنَّ ٱلَّذِىٓ أَحْيَاهَا لَمُحْىِ ٱلْمَوْتَىٰٓۚ إِنَّهُۥ عَلَىٰ كُلِّ شَىْءٍ قَدِيرٌ ۝

Technically, khushu' refers to a person's heart standing before the Lord and in submissiveness and subservience. And most importantly, focusing only on Him.

It is also said that khushu' is to submit to the truth, however, the truth is that, this is one of its results. Therefore, amongst the signs of khushu' is that when the servant opposes the truth and is reminded of it, he accepts and willing returns to it.

It is said that khushu' is the abating of the flames of lusts in the servants' breast and the dissipation of their smoke; replacing in their stead the blaze of the greatness of Allah in the heart.

Junaid said: Khushu' is the humbling of hearts to the One who knows the unseen."

The Gnostics have agreed that the seat of khushu' is the heart and that its fruits sprout on the limbs and they display it. The Prophet, peace and blessings be upon him, saw a man playing with his beard while praying and remarked: "If the heart of this person was humble, so too would his limbs be."

The Prophet, peace and blessings be upon him, said: "Taqwa is here," pointing to his breast. The Prophet, peace and blessings be upon, then said it three times. One of the Gnostics said: "Fine conduct on the outer is a clear indication of fine conduct on the inward."

One of them saw a person showing khushu' on his shoulders and body and said: "O such-and-such, khushu' is here," pointing to his breast, 'not here,' pointing to his shoulders.

One of the Companions, Hudhayfah, would say: "Take refuge with Allah from hypocritical khushu'." When asked what it was, he replied: "That you see the body humble and submissive while the heart is not."

'Umar (RA) saw a person with his neck bowed in prayer and said: "Such-and-such raise your head for khushu lies not on the neck but in the heart."

A'ishah (RA) saw some youth trying to walk with an air of quietude, so she asked: "Who are they?"

Her colleagues replied, "Ascetics."

She said: "When 'Umar walked, he walked rapidly; when he spoke, he was heard; when he struck someone, it hurt; when he fed (the poor), he made sure they ate to their fill; he was the true ascetic!"

Fudayl ibn Iyad said: "It used to be disliked for a person to display more khushu than was in his heart."

Hudhayfah said: "The first thing you will lose of your religion will be khushu and the last thing you will lose of your religion will be the prayer, and it is well possible that there is no good in a person who prays, and soon will come a time when you shall enter a large Masjid and not see a single person with khushu."

Sahl said: "The person whose heart has khushu will not go near Shaytan."

"We should know that Allah has created us to live an eternal life with no death, a life of pride and ease with no humiliation, a life of security with no fear, a life of richness with no poverty, a life of joy with no pain, a life of perfection with no flaws. Allah is testing us in this world with a life that will end in death, a life of pride that is accompanied by humiliation and degradation, a life that is tainted by fear, where joy and ease are mixed with sorrow and pain."

APPENDIX II

Ibn al-Qayyim on Hypocritical Khushu

The difference between "true" khushu engendered by faith and the hypocritical khushu is that the former takes place in the heart to Allah and is conduced by veneration, magnification, sobriety, dignity, and shyness.

The heart breaks for Allah, combining dread, bashfulness, love, and shyness with the perception of Allah's blessings and one's own transgressions. This necessarily engenders khushu in the heart which is then followed by khushu on the limbs.

Hypocritical khushu, on the other hand, appears on the limbs; it is a mere pretense, the person affecting something that is not there since the heart is void of khushu. One of the Companions would say: "I take refuge with Allah from hypocritical khushu." When asked what it was, he replied: "That you see the body humble and submissive while the heart is not."

The one who has khushu for the sake of Allah is a servant, in the breast of whom the flames of desires have abated and their smoke has dissipated, replacing in their stead radiance. The blaze of the greatness (of Allah) has been ignited, and the lusts of the soul have died in the face of fear and sobriety which have, in turn, stilled the limbs and quietened the heart. The heart is content and at peace with Allah, and it remembers Him; engulfed in the effusion of tranquility descending from its Lord, it becomes meek and humble.

The heart which is meek is the heart which is at peace and rest for the land which is low-lying to which water flows and settles. The same applies to the heart: when it is humble, i.e. it has achieved khushu, it becomes like this piece of low-laying land to which water flows and settles.

The sign of such a heart is that its owner will prostrate before Allah out of magnification and abject humility, broken before Him, never (desiring) to raise his head till the day he meets Him. This is the khushu engendered by faith.

The arrogant heart, on the other hand, heaves and swells in its arrogance like a fast flowing river. It is like an elevated portion of the land at which water never settles.

This is hypocritical khushu: the person feigns quietude and affects stillness of limb by way of ostentation. In reality, his soul is raging with lusts and desires; outwardly he display khushu, but inwardly the valley serpent and jungle lion lurk between his shoulders, waiting to pounce on the prey.

"There are no means of attaining faith and certainty except through the Qur'an."

"Women are one half of society which gives birth to the other half so it is as if they are the entire society."

"Had Allah lifted the veil for his slave and shown him how He handles his affairs for him, and how Allah is more keen for the benefit of the slave than his own self, his heart would have melted out of the love for Allah and would have been torn to pieces out of thankfulness to Allah. Therefore if the pains of this world tire you, do not grieve. For it may be that Allah wishes to hear your voice by way of Dua'a. So pour out your desires in prostration and forget about it and know; that verily Allah does not forget it."

"The ibtilaa' (testing) of the believer is like medicine for him. It cures him from illness. Had the illness remained it would destroy him or diminish his reward and level (in the hereafter). The tests and the trials extract these illnesses from him and prepare him for the perfect reward and the highest of degrees (in the life to come)."

"Sins have many side-effects. One of them is that they steal knowledge from you. There is no captive in a worse state than the one who is captivated by his worst enemy (Shaytan) and there is no prison which is tighter than the prison of hawa (desire) and there is no bond/fetter more strong than the bond of desire. How, then, will a heart which is captivated, imprisoned and fettered travel unto Allah and the Home of the Hereafter?"

"As long as you are performing prayer, you are knocking at the door of Allah, and whoever is knocking at the door of Allah, Allah will open it for him."

"When a person spends his entire day with no concern but Allah alone, Allah will take care of all his needs and take care of all that is worrying him; He will empty his heart so that it will be filled only with love for Him."

-- Ibn Qayyim Al-Jawziyya

www.ingramcontent.com/pod-product-compliance
Lightning Source LLC
Chambersburg PA
CBHW052204090526
44583CB00015BA/1543